1991

READING COMPREHENSION ASSESSMENT:
A Cognitive Basis

Peter H. Johnston
State University of New York at Albany

ila

International Reading Association
800 Barksdale Road   Newark, Delaware

Copyright 1983 by the
International Reading Association
Library of Congress Cataloging in Publication Data
Johnston, Peter H.
    Reading comprehension assessment

    Bibliography: p.
    1. Reading comprehension—Evaluation.   I. Title.
LB1050.45.J65   1983   428.4'3   82-12640
ISBN 0-87207-951-1

Contents

iii

Foreword

Existing reading tests in general and tests of reading comprehension in particular have tended to be heavy on test theory and statistics and light on reading and cognitive theory. The net results, as the authors of this IRA monograph say, are tests which are loaded on some general factor using items that discriminate between individuals but which are not derived from some articulate conceptualization of what reading comprehension is or how it should be evaluated for particular purposes.

This monograph is one attempt to approach the whole issue of assessing reading comprehension from a rational view. First, it considers what reading comprehension is; second, it addresses what factors influence it and its assessment such as text and reader characteristics. Third, it puts assessment methodology in the context of purposes and constraints. And, finally, it considers alternatives within the framework of what can and should be assessed.

In education, there are many decisions made at a number of levels purely on the basis of performance on reading tests. Pupils, programs, and teachers—in fact, entire school systems—are judged by gain scores on reading tests. Research studies support or reject hypotheses on the basis of reading tests scores. That means that any weakness or deficiency in the tests is reflected in weakeness in decisions and judgments based on them. Yet, Burros* reports that the majority of reading tests ever published are still in print, still in use, still making money for their publishers.

Works such as this monograph are important as they bring new knowledge to bear on assessment of reading comprehension. Perhaps we are on the threshold of a new era in reading assessment in which we will insist that assessment instruments have a basis in theory and research, clear purposes, and safeguards against misuse/abuse.

*Buros, O. *Reading tests and reviews*. Highland Park, New Jersey: Gryphon Press, 1968.

Kenneth S. Goodman
University of Arizona

Preface

This volume represents an attempt to draw together experimental and theoretical information which is relevant to the problems of assessing children's reading comprehension. Although the literature review is not exhaustive, it does draw on work from a number of disciplines.

In my opinion, the biggest contribution of basic research to the assessment of reading comprehension is the increased understanding of the objective of the assessment: Comprehension. I have made an attempt to resolve some of the conflicts which have beset reading comprehension assessment, and to draw out the implications for future study and application.

I owe considerable thanks to several of my colleagues: George McConkie, David Pearson, Bob Linn, Andrew Ortony, and Peter Winograd. I also owe thanks to NIE grant HEW-NIE-C-400-76-0116 which supported most of the work while I was at the Center for the Study of Reading, University of Illinois at Champaign-Urbana.

PJ

Introduction

In a hall a large group of children are seated at desks working feverishly on optical scan papers. An adult paces up and down the aisles, pausing occasionally, and constantly keeping an eye on the clock on the wall.

In a small laboratory, a child is seated in front of a CRT screen which displays segments of text. His head is held tightly in place. The experimenter stands close by and a computer in the background flashes a group of small lights.

In a classroom, a teacher and a child discuss a book which the child has just read. The teacher is asking the child many questions. The noise level in the classroom gradually increases.

What these three scenarios have in common is that they are all concerned with the assessment of reading comprehension. People assess reading comprehension for a wide variety of reasons under a variety of different circumstances, each with a different set of constraints. Assessment has been fraught with problems, a considerable number of which have stemmed from the lack of a coherent theoretical framework, especially one enabling understanding of exactly what reading comprehension is and what it involves. For example, the validity of tests, especially the diagnostic ones, is suspect since there is no complete model with which they can be compared. There is no rational method of test-item generation, and even attempts at item selection have so far been incomplete. Thus, the relationships among questions, text, and the act of reading have been ill-defined and unsystematic. While traditional measurement theory does give information for decisions about which of a set of items discriminates best between individuals, it does not help us select items that best differentiate component skills or that best measure the underlying construct of reading. It certainly does not help us to generate the items in the first place.

Lumsden (1976) claims that we appear to have approached the functional limits of mathematical and statistical sophistication in educational measurement. Tuinman (1979) argues similarily, presenting ample evidence to support the contention and claiming that test constructors have been saved from total embarrassment only by the fact that most tests load heavily on a general verbal factor.

Tuinman has also amassed evidence to show that attempts at forming and validating skill hierarchies have failed miserably. He states that "every teacher knows that it is possible to ask an easy 'higher order' question and a very difficult 'lower order' question" (p. 40). The tests bear little relationship to the actual societal reading demands, and since interpretation is not clear from the test development, tests are open to misuse and abuse. Recent research may help us in our attempts to solve some of these difficult problems.

This publication is an attempt to draw together experimental and theoretical information which is relevant to the problems of assessing children's reading comprehension. The goal is to present the implications of recent research for the assessment of reading comprehension.

One cannot readily cleave the problem of reading comprehension assessment into independent subproblems since the interrelationships among the different aspects are many and complex. However, this volume will be divided in the following manner. In order to address the assessment of reading comprehension, there must first be some agreement on how to define the object of our measurement, since the method and criteria of assessment must be governed by one's conception of the dimensions of the object of assessment. An attempt will then be made to delineate the various factors which will influence the outcome of our assessment. Consequently, the first two sections present and support a model of reading comprehension which integrates some previously opposed perspectives.

Having described reading comprehension and the various factors affecting it, the methodological problems of gathering useful assessment data will be dealt with, and some alternative approaches suggested. A further section will address the question of why one might want to assess reading comprehension. Finally, a summary will be presented and some implications for reading comprehension assessment will be suggested.

Chapter One

Defining Reading Comprehension

Introduction

Attempting to define reading comprehension is always a bold move—dissenters are likely to be many. Yet it is a problem which must be addressed since, if we cannot agree on what we are measuring, it seems unlikely that we will obtain any consensus on how to measure it. *It is in this area of reading comprehension assessment—understanding the nature of comprehension itself—that most progress has been made over the past few years.* In order to demonstrate this impact, old and new perspectives on some important issues will be contrasted.

The Relationship between Comprehension and Reading

Some Theoretical Issues

To begin with, *reading* will be considered as any reader interaction with text. Comprehension is *one aspect* of reading—the one with which we are concerned here. Other aspects include decoding, scanning (e.g., telephone directory use), and vocalizing the print on the page (word calling). This means that assessment of decoding is not here considered as part of assessment of comprehension except insofar as it might be predictive of problems with reading comprehension. This is not to say that decoding (in its general sense) is not a necessary prerequisite for reading comprehension, and interactively involved with it. Almost certainly, it is both of these.

In attempting to develop a definition of reading comprehension, the first issue to be addressed is whether reading comprehension should be viewed as a process or as a product. That is, should it be viewed as the change in (or state of) knowledge which has occurred through reading, or as the process by which the change (or state) comes about? A second issue relates to the nature of the process(es) involved in comprehension. Are there identifiable subsystems operating, or is there one complex indivisible process operating? A conceptualization of reading comprehension and how it helps us toward a resolution of these issues will then be examined.

Comprehension: A Process or a Product?

Most current approaches to the assessment of reading comprehension embody an assumption that reading comprehension is a product of a reader's interaction with a text. This product is stored in the reader's memory and may be examined by convincing the reader to express relevant segments of the stored material. Such an approach is less of a theoretical than a pragmatic attempt to find out how the interaction has changed the reader's knowledge. The process(es) involved in getting there are given less emphasis than the final product (i.e., the contents of memory). The product position implies that long-term memory plays a large part in comprehension, determining how "successful" the reader is at comprehending; this position is typified by standardized tests and free recall measures.

In contrast, Carroll (1971) contends that comprehension is a process which occurs immediately on reception of information and that only short-term memory is involved. Consequently, he states, "As soon as longer time intervals are involved in the testing of comprehension, there is the possibility that we are studying memory processes along with, or in place of, comprehension processes" (p. 6). Carroll's "processes" are represented by eye-movement and reaction-time studies, and miscue analysis.

Royer and Cunningham (1978, p. 36) take issue with both the process and product approaches and contend that "...comprehension processes and memory processes are inextricably intertwined....We assume that a comprehended message will be retained in memory better than an uncomprehended message. There is ample evidence to support this assumption (Bransford & Johnson, 1972; Bransford & Johnson,

1973; Dooling & Lachman, 1971)." Indeed, Bower (1978, p. 212) states "Superior memory seems to be an incidental byproduct of fully understanding a text." This indicates a blend of the concerns of both product and process approaches, an interest in the memorial outcome *and* the process(es) of attaining it. However, should we construe this blend as being a fact of biology or a flaw in our assessment? That is, are memorial, retrieval, and comprehension processes truly inextricably interwoven, or is it just that we have difficulty assessing them independently?

These three theoretical positions have produced a good deal of friction in the assessment world. The last of the three positions approximates the position which will be presented and justified in this paper.

Comprehension: Divisible or Indivisible?

Reading comprehension has alternately been considered as a holistic process (Drahozal & Hanna, 1978; Thorndike, 1974) and as a process composed of distinct subprocesses (Davis, 1972). The skills or component approach to reading comprehension is based on the assumption that comprehension can be analyzed into various discrete subprocesses, all of which are necessary for successful performance of mature reading. Further, it is assumed that if a child lacks the skills, then specific remedial training can correct the difficulty. On the other hand, proponents of a holistic view of reading comprehension contend that one cannot break down into components what the mind does. This is a much more pressing, difficult, and deep-seated issue than the process/product issue because it has even more powerful consequences for teaching and remediation.

In the following discussion, *subskills* and *subprocesses* will be used in the broad sense and somewhat interchangeably.

The basic arguments. Many different sets of "necessary and sufficient" subskills of reading have been derived by logical analysis (Baker & Stein, 1978; Rystrom, 1970; Vernon, 1962) with considerable lack of agreement on the matter. However, the major approach to isolating such skills has been through factor analysis. Davis (1944) presented a rational and statistical analysis of a study claiming eight separate subskills. He reanalyzed his data on several occasions and still claimed small amounts of unique variance accounted for after the first major factor (Davis, 1968, 1972). Reanalysis of Davis' data by Spearitt (1972) indicated four separate factors: recalling word meanings; drawing inferences; recognizing author's purpose, attitude, tone, and mood; and following the passage structure. Studies by Bateman, Frandsen, and Dedmon (1964), Drahozal and Hanna (1978), and others have found variety both in type and number of factors, and little consensus on either.

Proponents of the single factor (holistic) concept have used similar empirical techniques to demonstrate opposite conclusions (Clark, 1972; Thorndike, 1974; Derrick, Note 1). However, the main proponent of the holistic approach has been Thorndike (1974, p. 57) who claims "The barrier...[is]...not primarily a deficit of one or more specific and readily teachable reading skills but is a reflection of generally meager intellectual processes." Thorndike uses a variety of data to support his contention that reading is in fact reasoning and cannot be decomposed into separate elements.

Problems with the subskills/holistic research. A number of problems have been associated with the research used to substantiate the subskills and holistic positions, aside from the common arguments over types of communality chosen and rotation used in the factor analyses. These problems have made it difficult to adequately defend either position, and they include the following:

1. The test passages appear to have been arbitrarily chosen.
2. Analyses have been across different age groups. However, different skills may be important at different ages, and different items may be interpreted in developmentally different ways (Stein & Glenn, 1978).
3. Items have been selected on the basis of their capacity to discriminate among individuals rather than their capacity to differentiate separate skills.
4. The word knowledge factor probably represents global world knowledge.
5. Factor analysis depends on item intercorrelations and these depend on variance of the traits in the

sample. If there is one trait and small variance, one can get a number of unstable factors. But if the traits measured are correlated, and subject variances on the traits are large, then the first factor smothers the others. This is almost bound to occur given the facts expressed in points 3 and 4. Also, if the items are hierarchical set (as is indicated by Davis, 1972, and even showing up in Thorndike's 1974 results), subjects able to answer higher level questions should be able to answer lower level questions. Thus, if there is good variation in the subjects' abilities, then inter-item correlations will be high and, again, the first factor will dominate (Andrich & Godfrey, 1978-1979).

6. The search has been directed at finding independent skills and there seems to be no reason to suppose that different reading comprehension skills should be uncorrelated. Indeed, interfacilitation of subskills has been indicated by Guthrie (1973).

These problems are not restricted to the factor-analytic approaches to the location of subskills. For example, Andrich and Godfrey (1978-79), used a single-logistic model rather than a factor-analytic model. With Davis' data they located four hierarchical subskills which differ from the other analyses but which still lack logical or intuitive appeal.

Part of the problem here is that without a theory that can guide the search for identifiable subskills, it has been difficult to get a feeling for the level at which to look for them. For example, "main idea finding" is a popular conception of a subskill, but so is "word knowledge." However, if we look more carefully at the nature of the comprehension task, we may find (as is argued below) that we have been looking for the subskills in the wrong places.

It is clear that it would be useful to know of a set of remediable subskills which comprise reading comprehension. This would provide a framework for effective assessment and remediation of reading comprehension difficulties. If we are to locate such a set we must conduct a search that is driven by theory rather than by solely pragmatic concerns. Thus we must begin to elaborate a coherent theoretical model of reading comprehension.

An Emerging Perspective on Reading Comprehension

Recently there have been some basic changes in our conception of reading comprehension. However, these have not yet been reflected in our assessment procedures. In 1971, Carroll posed three questions for researchers. He asked

> ...whether it is possible in fact to distinguish "pure" comprehension of language texts from processes of inferences, deduction, and problem solving that often accompany the reception of language. An empirical question would be to see whether it would be possible to decrease the correlation of comprehension ability tests with intelligence tests by eliminating or reducing those elements of comprehension tests that call for inferential processes that go beyond sheer comprehension. ...Research is needed to see to what extent it is possible to reduce their dependence on memory. (p. 3)

In the past eight years, much of the appropriate research has been done, and the result has been that the original questions are no longer relevant. For example, Pearson and Johnson (1978) contend that

> Comprehension is building bridges between the new and the known.... Comprehension is active not passive; that is, the reader cannot help but interpret and alter what he reads in accordance with prior knowledge about the topic under discussion. Comprehension is not simply a matter of recording and reporting verbatim what has been read. Comprehension involves a great deal of inference making. (p. 24)

The contrast between these quotes by Carroll and Pearson and Johnson indicates the recent changes in our conceptions of what comprehension is. While there is still some willingness to separate inferencing and problem solving, they are no longer generally considered to be removable from the comprehension process, but rather are considered an integral part of it, like the apple in apple pie. One must even infer the intended meanings of single words in context (especially polysemous words like "run"). Indeed, the status of inference has shifted over the past few years from a single process, almost an optional extra, to a selection of fairly well-differentiated types of inference upon which virtually all comprehension is predicted.

We do not consider readers to have comprehended something if they can give only a rote recall of the elements. We consider that readers have comprehended a text only when they have established logical connections among the ideas in the text and can express these in an alternate form. In this way, inferences are critical acts of comprehension, since they allow us to make various words meaningful, join together propositions and sentences, and fill in the missing chunks of information.

Pace (Note 2) has pointed out that in familiar story situations there is a difference between "active" and "passive" inferencing, passive inferencing being a matter of merely recognizing the appropriate schema. Thus it is clear that the common "inference question" is no longer a single question type. Indeed, many literal questions may involve inferencing, especially at the lexical level. We must consider what type of cognitive process was involved, based on our growing understanding of these processes.

Trabasso (1980) has pointed out that the functions which these inferences perform are fourfold:

1. resolution of lexical ambiguity;
2. resolution of pronominal and nominal references;
3. establishment of context for the sentence;
4. establishment of larger framework for interpretation, i.e., a model base for top-down processing.

These functions are here ordered from bottom-up to top-down in terms of the processes which they involve. Top-down processing requires a previously formed knowledge structure which already contains the major relationships. This is conceived of as a "slot-filling" activity. That is, the appropriate knowledge structures already exist; only the specifics need to be filled in. In the case of absence of such a structure (or the failure to use it) the reader must rely more on bottom-up processing, which requires more use of lexical and linguistic knowledge and word recognition to build meaning sentence by sentence. The reader can then proceed to build a higher order structure.

Warren, Nicholas, and Trabasso (1979) have a more detailed analysis of inferencing in terms of what the inferences do. They can be slot-filling if they generate extra information which was not actually in the text. For example, if the text gives "James flew to New York," one infers that James first went to the airport, entered the plane, and so forth. Learning that James went to the airport in a taxi is merely providing expected information, since there is already a "slot" for such information. If the information is not provided, we provide it ourselves. Alternatively, inferences can be text-connecting if they establish connective relationships between elements of text. There are a number of subclasses of inferences, independent of the text-based classification as slot-filling or text-connecting. These are:

1. Logical relationships:
   a. Motivational. For example, the text says "Bill had not eaten in two days." One is likely to infer from that a certain motivation on Bill's part to find some food.
   b. Enablement. One can infer without difficulty that wealth enables purchasing of things.
   c. Psychological cause. One could readily infer, given the appropriate background, that one person's hatred could have been the cause of another's death.
   d. Physical cause. One can infer that an ice-laden road caused a car to skid.
2. Informational relationships:
   a. Spatial and temporal. Given that A occurred before B, it can be inferred that B occurred after A.
   b. Pronominal and lexical. One knows the referent of "he" in a sentence, and which meaning of "run" is intended.
3. Evaluation. Inferences which are based on moral and social judgment (John beats his wife; therefore, he is not a nice person).

Such inferences are the very essence of reading comprehension and the more inferences readers make, generally, the more they comprehend. For example, Omanson, Warren, and Trabasso (1978) found that by giving children clear information on a protagonist's goals, thus allowing more inferences to be made, the children showed greater comprehension of the stories. This is not to say, however, that the reader is to generate all possible inferences. This would lead to a complete loss of the author's message. The reader, rather, has a system for directing inferencing. This system seems to utilize a concept of "good form" such that what an author leaves out of a text, and what a reader is allowed to add, are governed by some implicit canonical forms and Gricean-type rules (Adams & Bruce, 1980).

It is likely that inferencing is initially fairly text-based but that good readers quickly shift to a more model-based generation of inferences. That is, since often there are many possible inferences, inferencing processes must be somewhat selective. It seems that we try to get a jump ahead of the text by inferring where it is leading us, building a mental model of what we think it is about. Our model produces questions which need to be answered (slots to be filled) and as we answer these there are fewer alternatives for other questions, and new questions arise. If we find an answer or another piece of information which does not fit our model, we have to examine the assumptions which we have made in constructing our model.

These processes are conceived of as the reader's active interaction with a specific text, given his or her background knowledge, and within the context of a given task and a given social setting. This conception will be elaborated throughout the book.

In a nutshell then, reading comprehension is viewed as the process of using the cues provided by the author and one's prior knowledge to infer the author's intended meaning. This involves a considerable amount of inferencing at all levels as one builds a model of the meaning of the text. If prior knowledge is strong, then a detailed model may be rapidly constructed which reduces the reading to slot-filling and verifying, and inferences to mere default values in the model (elaborated in the next chapter).

Toward a Resolution of the Issues

The theoretical perspective presented can be substantiated and elaborated further using evidence from several recent theoretical and experimental sources. Through this elaboration I intend to demonstrate that earlier research and conceptions of reading comprehension were restrictive. Those few researchers who considered reading comprehension in the context of general cognitive abilities were hampered by the lack of adequate research on cognitive skills.

Considering reading as a specific application of more general cognitive processing skills and strategies enables us to propose some resolutions to the theoretical issues presented earlier in this paper. For example, the conflict between the subskills approach and Thorndike's claim (1974) that reading is, in fact, reasoning, and therefore not a series of subskills, can be reduced by recognizing that reasoning is not an indivisible ability. Thus, while reading may well be reasoning, that does not preclude it from having subskills.

Reasoning Strategies in Reading

Several lines of research indicate that reasoning is not a unitary ability. Seigler (in press), in studying children's problem-solving behavior, looked at the strategies children used to solve various problems. He was able to analyze the strategies used and diagnose and correct problems with them. Recent work by Sternberg (1977) also indicates that one can define a series of strategies for answering various I.Q. test questions. Furthermore, training subjects in the use of these strategies leads to great improvements in performance. Similar results have been noted by Pellegrino and Glaser (in press).

That reading involves reasoning is apparent from a number of studies in artificial intelligence (e.g., Schank & Abelson, 1977; Wilensky, Note 3) and reading comprehension (e.g., Collins, Brown, & Larkin, 1977; Collins & Smith, 1980). The direction of research is now toward making explicit the reasoning strategies involved in reading comprehension.

There are two general levels of strategy which can be described. The first set of strategies is involved with helping the reader construct a model of the meaning of the text from the information available in the text and in the reader's head. The second set is that by which readers monitor their progress toward understanding the text, detecting lapses in comprehension, and initiating strategies to rectify the difficulties.

Strategies involving cue use and model building. Rosenblatt (1978) has convincingly argued that the writer's intended meaning is ultimately unknowable. I contend, however, that readers do attempt to discover what the author intended to convey. Therefore, reading comprehension, at the basic level, involves the use of the textual clues to create a model of the presumed meaning of a text. There is a wide variety of cues and information available to assist readers in their attempts to construct the meaning of the symbols on the page. Information is available from the reader's head (background knowledge), sometimes from the social setting, and from the page. The information takes certain systematic forms, and there are many different relationships between the information sources.

Meyer's (1975) and Clements' (1976) work indicates that good readers are aware of different types of macrosignals within the text. Macrosignals are cue systems which give information about the organization of the information on the page. Brown and Day's work (Note 4) shows that readers can be made aware of other structural aspects of text such as repetition and elaboration. An analysis of several other important cue systems has been presented by Collins and Smith (1980). (See the section on Text in the chapter that follows.) Readers can use such sources of information to construct their model of the text meaning and to evaluate it. Collins, Brown, and Larkin (1977) present some of the strategies which readers use to do this:

1. Rebinding. If the interpretation of the last piece read causes a conflict in the model, then keep all of the model to date but find a new interpretation for the last bit.
2. Question default interpretation. The question here is, "Is X a standard X with standard properties?"
3. Questioning a direct or indirect conflict. For example, a chain of inferences leads one to a conflict with another part of the model, which forces one to return and question an earlier inference in the chain.

4. Near or distant shift of focus. The reader reaches a problem which he cannot solve, so tries to answer a different question.
5. Case analysis and most likely case assignment. Readers sometimes fill in with guesses and then check to see whether the consequent constraints allow convergent solution.

In using the above strategies to evaluate their models, readers also have certain conditions for acceptance or rejection of the total model. They check (generally unconsciously):

1. the plausibility of the assumptions and consequences of the model;
2. the completeness of the model;
3. the interconnectedness of the model; and
4. the match of the model with the text.

That is to say, in testing the model, readers seem to check its predictive power, whereas it is constructed by checking on the fit with prior data.

Kintch and van Dijk (1978) presented a theoretical conception of how information is processed while reading and used variation in some of the model's parameters to account for individual differences in recall. The model includes a set of summarization strategies. Brown and Day (1980) analyzed the think-aloud protocols of proficient summarizers and validated a similar set of strategies. These researchers then taught children and adults the strategies for finding the gist of a passage and found that the subjects' ability to summarize improved immensely. They essentially found that people look for certain information and then initiate a processing strategy based on what they find. Some examples are, "Is there a topic sentence for this paragraph? No? Then construct one. Is this information repeated? Yes? Then delete it."

Brown and Day's work indicates that by instructing readers on the appropriate information checklist and rules to use, readers' summaries can be improved. While these strategies are initially used consciously, Brown and Day found that experts at summarizing used the strategies without being aware of doing so. Some children consistently used some strategies but not others, and some of the strategies appeared to be more difficult than others. These facts tend to demonstrate that Brown and Day's work dealt with the use of separate strategies, or cognitive skills. Thus it seems that what had been one of the few intuitively appealing subskills, "finding the main point," may actually break down into several lower-level strategies which are separable and teachable. More will be said about these issues when we consider the task demands of different types of reading.

Given this conceptualization of reading comprehension, it is eminently clear why there are such high correlations between tests of reading comprehension and tests of reasoning. Reading comprehension does have a large reasoning component.

Strategies involving comprehension monitoring. There has recently been a great deal of research into comprehension monitoring or "metacomprehension" (e.g., Baker, 1979; Brown, 1978; Markman, 1979; Winograd & Johnston, 1980).

Comprehension failure can occur at the word, sentence, intersentence, or discourse level. At each level there is the problem of being unable to locate a reasonable interpretation, or of having several possible interpretations. At the discourse level, one can also fail to get the point or fail to understand some section in relation to another section. What is required in comprehension monitoring is awareness of the triggering conditions and symptoms of comprehension failure, and awareness of the strategies which can be used to remedy the situation. Collins and Smith (1980), in presenting some of these strategies, also point out that each repair strategy carries a cost, since it either diverts the reader's attention from the main thread, or it puts the reader in danger of failing to understand a larger segment of the text. Some of the strategies for dealing with comprehension failure are:

1. ignore and read on;
2. suspend judgment;
3. form a tentative hypothesis;
4. reread the current sentence;
5. reread the previous context;
6. go to an expert source.

The use of these strategies will obviously depend upon the purpose for which the reader is reading. For example, a reader reading for gist will be more inclined to "ignore and read on" than to "reread the current sentence."

The Relationship between Reading and Background Knowledge

Invariably, factor-analytic studies of reading comprehension have found a word knowledge factor on which comprehension tests load highly. In studies of readability, too, any index of vocabulary difficulty accounts for about 80 percent of the predicted variance (Coleman, 1971). Models of reading comprehension must account for these facts.

Anderson and Freebody (1979) have examined the three competing hypotheses which attempt to explain this finding: instrumentalist, aptitude, and background knowledge. The instrumentalist position is that knowing words allows text comprehension and not knowing them means that the reader cannot adequately proceed through the text. The aptitude hypothesis, a holistic approach, considers vocabulary knowledge as just another index of verbal IQ, which is the real factor accounting for comprehension. The knowledge hypothesis suggests that vocabulary knowledge is a secondary index of the extent of background conceptual frameworks (schemata). While data are not available to allow us to choose among these three hypotheses, the knowledge hypothesis is most consistent with the theoretical framework developed thus far. The more background knowledge the reader possesses, the more likely it is that the reader knows the relevant words, and the more likely he or she will be able to make appropriate inferences while reading, and to build appropriate models of meaning. Indeed, Spiro (1980) has proposed a series of "subskills" which derive from a schema-theoretic notion of reading comprehension. This approach takes into consideration the use of background knowledge and the integration with background knowledge of what is derived from the text.

Spiro's analysis arrives at the following possibly distinct areas:

1. schema availability, i.e., presence or absence of background knowledge;
2. schema selection, i.e., decisions on the selection of an appropriate schema to which to fit the data;
3. schema maintenance, i.e., maintaining activation of the selected schemata while proceeding through the text;

4. schema instantiation and refinement, i.e., using the appropriate schema to organize data and refine the model which one is building to fit the data;
5. schema combination, i.e., integration of different sets of knowledge;
6. nonanalytic aspects of schema based processing, i.e., the subjective feelings associated with processing.

This approach is not in conflict with the notions presented above; rather, it complements them. For example, the Kintch and van Dijk (1978) model requires schematic knowledge in order to operate effectively. Such knowledge aids in reducing the short-term memory load in the model since information can be transferred more rapidly from short-term memory to long-term memory, and can be stored in larger chunks (Chi, 1977).

Spiro's model contains concepts of schema availability and schema selection or access. Schema availability refers to the problem of lack of the requisite background information about a specific area, whereas the problem of schema selection refers to the failure to use available background knowledge when it is required.

Other subskills Spiro presents represent the strategic use of available information. For example, schema selection has been looked upon as a teachable skill by Winograd and Johnston (1980). The evidence suggests that provided the schema is present in the first place, selection is a learnable skill. Some children do not relate what they read to their background knowledge but can be taught to do so (Hansen, 1981). Spiro (1980) also suggests that updating old schemata rather than continually attempting to construct new ones is a skill which a child does not necessarily bring to reading. Schema maintenance is important too, since the reader must often maintain certain referents in working memory in order to maintain coherence.

Bransford (1979) has provided a good illustration of the effects of teaching children strategies for schema use in reading. Children who used these strategies exhibited excellent recall in contrast to those who did not use them. Furthermore, children taught to use the strategies were able to improve their recall considerably.

The upshot of this work on prior knowledge via schema theory is that the large correlations between reading comprehension tests and vocabulary tests are quite predictable. If vocabulary is simply indicative of background knowledge, then limited vocabulary would indicate a limited ability to make the appropriate inferences and build the models of meaning which allow more efficient top-down reading.That is, the reasoning component of reading would be restricted by the lack of available data to solve the puzzles in the text. On the other hand, more reasoning skill would be required to make the text coherent.

Brown, Campione, and Day (1980) have distinguished between these three important types of knowledge: strategic, content, and metacognitive. Strategic knowledge refers to the repertoire of rules, procedures, tricks, and routines for making learning a more efficient activity (Brown, 1975). Content or factual knowledge refers to information that learners have concerning the subject under consideration and their general knowledge of the world (Anderson, 1977; Brown, 1975; Chi, 1977). Metacognitive knowledge refers to the information that learners have concerning the state of their own knowledge base and the task demands they are facing (Baker & Brown, 1980; Brown, 1975; Flavell & Wellman, 1977).

This distinction links the present section on prior knowledge with the previous section on reasoning subskills, since it is clear that a reader must have knowledge of appropriate strategies but may or may not make use of the knowledge. It also introduces a further component, that of knowledge about the demands of the task to be engaged in. That this is related to reading failure has been shown by Myers and Paris (1978) and Canney and Winograd (1979). For example, children may be unaware that the purpose of reading is to gain information from text, or that it is necessary to use what they already know in order to understand the text.

Summary

Our concept of reading comprehension has changed quite radically over the past few years, along with our methods of studying it. It is hypothesized that knowledge is stored in schematic structures (Anderson, Spiro, & Anderson, 1977; Rumelhart & Ortony, 1977), and *comprehension* is the process(es) involved in forming, elaborating, modifying or integrating these knowledge structures (Rumelhart, 1977). Degree of comprehension of a text can be considered in terms of the creation, modification, elaboration and integration of the relevant knowledge structures. That is, it refers to the extent to which the information conveyed by the discourse is represented in these cognitive structures. But more than that, it refers to the extent of the interrelationships among and within the structures. (This is not restricted to factual information but includes emotive information also.)

Reading comprehension is considered to be a complex behavior which involves conscious and unconscious use of various strategies, including problem-solving strategies, to build a model of the meaning which the writer is assumed to have intended. The model is constructed using schematic knowledge structures and the various cue systems which the writer has given (e.g., words, syntax, macrostructures, social information) to generate hypotheses which are tested using various logical and pragmatic strategies. Most of this model must be inferred, since text can never be fully explicit and, in general, very little of it is explicit because even the appropriate intensional and extensional meanings of words must be inferred from their context.

In addition to the reasoning processes, good readers monitor the progress of their comprehension, and use repair strategies when necessary. This also requires that they decide, on the basis of their purpose for reading, when to remove their processing from "automatic pilot," take conscious control, and instigate the appropriate alternative strategies—a very important aspect of reading comprehension.

The position largely resolves the issue of viewing reading as reasoning versus as a series of subskills. However, by demonstrating that, in fact, reasoning itself has subskills, the two positions are not incompatible. Reading can be reasoning and have subskills at the same time.

The position does not, however, fully resolve the process versus product debate, but rather places it in a different perspective, reducing its relevance somewhat. For the purpose of diagnosis, in particular, the problem is that we are stuck for the most part with *product* measures, when we are more interested in *processes*, since these are what we can influence through instruction. It seems that the two approaches to assessment (process and product) should not be dichotomized but rather should be considered complementary approaches to the same problem. This view is based on the assertion that elements of both process and product exist in many forms of assessment and that reading comprehension will be impeded by failure of processing, storage, or retrieval of information.

Since it is the processing aspects that educators can, in principle, alter through instruction (little can yet be done about storage per se), these become important objects of assessment. It is thus unfortunate that the most readily available forms of assessment are of the product type. However, it is clear that the processes of reading comprehension must utilize or act upon the already stored information, so we are forced to study process and product in their interaction. Indeed, this paper supports the position taken by Royer and Cunningham (1978) and holds that studying comprehension without studying memory is somewhat pointless. It is rather like contemplating the sound of the proverbial tree falling in the primeval forest. It is philosophically interesting but practically and psychologically of minimal interest.

The theoretical issues presented in this first section provide a base from which we can develop our understanding of what we are measuring and what such a measurement will mean. While this discussion is far from complete, the following sections will expand further some of the issues raised above.

One issue I have said little about thus far is what Spiro (1980) has called the "non-analytic" aspects of reading. Louise Rosenblatt (1978) distinguishes between two types of reading: efferent and aesthetic. Efferent reading (from the Latin *efferre*, meaning to carry away) focuses on what remains after reading. Aesthetic reading seems to correspond with Spiro's notion of non-analytic aspects of processing. Like virtually all of our reading comprehension instruction, our assessment of it addresses only the efferent aspect.

Bower (1978) has made some inroads into the area of the affective transaction between reader and text using post-hypnotic suggestion of mood; however, there is little other related research. What has been done can be interpreted within a schema-theoretic model which allows that affective data is bound up in the schemata in the same manner as factual information, and is accessed in a similar manner (as suggested at the beginning of this summary).

Aesthetic reading has a different purpose from that of efferent reading. In efferent reading, the attempt is to build a model of the author's intended meaning, whereas in aesthetic reading the intent is simply to experience a work of art. The model invoked in this latter type of reading is a very personal one, and it is not at all clear that assessment of it is appropriate: How should one interpret the outcome, and against what criteria should one compare it? Assessment may be antithetical to aesthetic reading in that assessment attempts may force the reader to read efferently so as to retain information to be used in a test, thus defeating the purpose of the assessment.

For the above reasons, I will not specifically address the theoretical and practical problems related to non-analytic reading. The interested reader should refer to Rosenblatt (1978) for an excellent introduction to the subject.

Chapter Two

Factors Which Influence Reading Comprehension and Its Assessment

Introduction

Assessment of reading comprehension requires interpretation of an individual's performance of some task which is based on information from a given text within a given context. Thus, performance on the test will depend on characteristics of the text, the nature of the task, and the context, as well as the person's reading abilities and prior knowledge. Consequently, it is necessary to understand the influence of these associated factors in order to make a meaningful interpretation of an individual's performance on assessment devices. In this section, I will discuss the various factors which influence reading comprehension and its assessment. These factors turn out to be excellent places for teachers and others to look to find explanations of children's real or apparent reading comprehension failures. The topics discussed are:

1. the text (its content, structure, and language);
2. the appropriateness of the text to the student's prior knowledge;
3. the sources of answers to questions;
4. the task demands of the assessment procedures.

The Text

If one has a selection of samples of different texts, it seems likely that the level of difficulty for a given reader will vary considerably across the texts. There are many possible causes for such variability in difficulty, and each potential cause is likely to differ in potency from reader to reader. A fair amount of research has been directed at isolating these variables.

The research has largely involved analyzing text to determine its readability. Though the work is not yet able to algorithmically improve prediction of readability, it can indicate to an extent why one piece is likely to be more difficult than another. However, some of this work is still rooted more in linguistics than in psycholinguistics, and thus is less concerned with the psychological reasons for reading difficulty. Also, much of this work is still pragmatically based rather than theoretically based. Text difficulty is currently defined in terms of either normative difficulty or readability formulae (regression prediction of normative difficulty), the latter being based on secondary criteria—pragmatic predictors such as sentence length or word frequency. These measures do not seem able to adequately distinguish between well-written, challenging texts and badly constructed texts which make interpretation difficult.

In order to select passages for assessment procedures, we need to know the characteristics of the passages—what makes one different from another. This is especially so if we wish to test children with a range of ability. Alas, the state of theoretical development in psychology and linguistics cannot support a definitive analysis of text at this point. This is, in fact, the objective of much current research, which is proceeding along two lines:

1. analysis of text in terms of its content and structure and the relationships between the two;
2. analysis of the writer/reader relationship, looking at text as a communicative device.

The import of these two approaches will be considered next.

Content/Structure Research

The characteristics of texts have been studied from the perspective of text as text (somewhat independent of the author). One aspect of text which affects what a reader recalls is the sheer quantity of information, as measured by passage length (Newsome & Gaite, 1971), density of information (Goetz, Anderson, & Schallert, 1979; Kintch & Keenan, 1973), and density of new information (Aiken, Thomas, & Shennum, 1975). Kintch, Kozmainsky, Streby, McKoon, and Keenan (1975) also have shown that the density of arguments in propositions slows reading and reduces recall. The more text content is concrete and imaginable (Paivio, 1971), and interesting (Johnson, 1974), the more memorable it is. Bower (1978) also shows that text can induce a reader to identify with a particular character, thus influencing recall.

The extent to which information is represented in the text (so that the reader does not have to infer it) has an effect on recall. McConkie (1978, p. 17) summarizes this:

> In general, textual manipulations which reduce information useful to the reader in building a coherent representation of the content can be expected to reduce comprehension of the passage. In some cases, the reader's prior knowledge will compensate for loss of textual information or relations may be identified on a problem solving basis requiring greater reading time.

This clearly indicates the importance of being able to specify, as far as possible, what is stated explicitly in the text, and what is only implied, especially if one intends to measure in what way the reader's knowledge changed as a result of his or her interaction with the text.

Specifying what must be inferred is especially important for developing test items and understanding performance on them, particularly the specific use of background knowledge. For example, there are developmental differences in children's contextual inference-making skills. Recall accuracy is highly correlated with these inferences, and increases with age (Paris & Upton, 1976).

Recently there has been considerable interest in analysis of narrative text. The commonality of elements in different narrative texts has given rise to a theory of *story grammars*. This theory posits the existence of conventionalized macrostructures derived from background knowledge of texts and the way things work in the world. That even young children are aware of such structures was shown by Brown and Murphy (1975). These experimenters found that four -year-olds recalled logical ordering of pictures better than random orderings. They also found that if the random orderings had a logical story built around them, recall improved. Thus it seems that even young children can use their knowledge of logical relations between things to help understand and recall information. A considerable amount of information has been accumulated on this form, some of which indicates differences between good and poor readers, and developmental differences.

Knowledge and use of these conventional macrostructures appear to facilitate text comprehension by allowing the reader to rapidly construct from the text a model of a possible world of situations which accounts for relationships within the text. These models have been described variously as frames (Minsky, 1975) or schemata (Rumelhart & Ortony, 1977) and are units of conventional knowledge which provide a basis for the organization of mutual expectations and interactions. These have given rise to the notion of "well-formedness" of text.

While young children possess such structures, they seem less able to use them to organize information. Brown and French (1976) found that preschoolers had more difficulty than older children in remembering sentences when the order in which the sentences were presented differed from the natural order of the events. Stein and Glenn (1978) showed that 5-year-olds are good at the recall of well-formed stories, and Stein and Glenn (Note 5) showed that children deal with systematic disruptions in the well-formedness of the stories in developmentally different ways.

There are cues in the text to these organizational structures, such as topic sentences; macroconnectors (but, however, and because); and discontinuities in time, location, actors, and content. Provided that a reader is aware of and knows what to do with them, these cues can assist him in his cognitive modelling of the text. Stein and Nezworski (1978) showed that fifth graders could recall structural disruptions at least as well as normal orderings if explicit markers were used. However, these markers were only partially helpful for first graders. It has also been shown (Marshall & Glock, 1978-1979) that, in the case of expository text, some readers are less influenced by the text structure than are others. More proficient adult readers are able to read text for their own purposes and can override such built-in emphases. This finding has implications for comprehension assessment: it would seem possible to determine whether a particular reader is sensitive to such structures, and whether he or she is able to override them.

A considerable amount is now known about the characteristics of narrative text, and some work has been done on the structure of expository text. It is more difficult to describe the macrostructures in expository text because the relationships among text segments are more diverse that those in the narrative. This is largely because of the greater variety of possible content matter. However, work by Clements (1976), Grimes (1975), and Meyer (1975) has shown that such rhetorical structures do exist in expository text and are used by people in their efforts to construct meaning.

These recent developments have given us greater direction in the area of text analysis. Story grammars have shown the kinds of inferences that people make in certain content/structure situations. In the case of narratives, the structural expectations which the reader develops are to a considerable extent dependent upon the text topic because of the reader's stored knowledge of the social situations and the normal descriptions of them.

Readers probably attempt to form a causal chain as a central core of a passage (Schank, 1975). Consequently, attributive information, which is normally not part of the causal chain, is not as well remembered as causal or action information, which is normally part of the chain. If attributive information, which is less important than causal information, is what is tested in reading comprehension tests (Tuinman, 1979) then it is important that we know what problems readers have in retrieving it.

On the other hand, if causal information is not stated in the text, it is normally inferred. Because it is stored as part of the causal chain, it is likely to be related or identified as having been stated explicitly. But because children are not always able to use such knowledge for top-down processing it is likely that the structure of their recall will differ from canonical forms.

Some further interesting relationships among structures, content, and comprehension assessment were found in a study by Freebody (1980). While he obtained data to show that prior knowledge and word difficulty independently influence reading comprehension, he also found that the order in which subjects read passages affected their comprehension of them. Specifically, he found that variations in cohesion were only effective when they occurred in texts read at the beginning or end of a series of three passages. Evidence of primacy and recency effects were also noted in subjects' performance, independent of the importance of the information. Clements (1976) obtained a similar effect also. This may be important information for the interpretation of current assessment devices which present the reader with a variety of brief passages.

There is little doubt, then, that variations in the structure of text are often related to content and that these variations have distinctive effects on different readers. Readers' failure to effectively deal with these structures and disruptions in them may indicate broader problems which they may face in their reading.

The Writer-Reader Relationship

The interaction between author and reader via the text, like all social interactions, is based on "good form," and in that way is consistent across texts, though the specific form may vary among different text types.

Beyond the work on narrative and rhetorical structures, work is being conducted by Cohen and others (Adams, Bruce, Cohen, Collins, Gentner, Rubin, Smith, Starr, Starr & Steinberg, Note 6) on the characteristics of instructional forms, and by Bruce (in press) on the broader, social aspects of text. Both are examining different aspects of text as they relate to writer-reader interactions.

In this approach the text is considered in its role as a communicative device. The author has a knowledge base, some of which (the passage base) he or she wishes to communicate to the reader. This passage base is frequently nonlinear in structure, yet the final text must be linear. For example, while the actual events being described originally occurred at the same time, they must be described consecutively. The author's task is to organize this message in light of what he or she perceives to be the characteristics of the reader, in terms of presumed background knowledge, possible goals, and so forth, to produce a text from which the reader will be likely to derive the intended meaning.

Cohen is attempting to specify the kinds of assumptions which both reader and writer make in their attempts to provide and gather information. He considers the expert-novice instructional interaction to be a special case of social interaction, and by varying the modality of communication, he is able to infer the assumptions which reader and writer make about one another. Reader and writer each attempt to estimate the other's goals and purposes.

Bruce (in press) has used a similar conception of reading as a communicative social interaction. This conception of reading allows us to consider certain dimensions of the text: participants, meaning, time, location, and physical text. It is possible to have interaction between author and reader, between character and character, and between levels of meaning, and interactions between each of these.

While considerable work has been done on the development of certain of the structures which occur in texts, less work has been done on the problem of constructing a broad system for text classification. Developing such a system is an essential project because, recognizing that different types of text tend to represent different tasks and different problems for the reader, we need to draw test passages from different domains of text and need to be able to specify the characteristics of the domains.

Bruce's work represents a good beginning in the development of a classification system. The work classifies narrative text with respect to a psychologically meaningful system based upon an awareness of social interactions. It also gives a key to what a reader needs to be aware of in order to attain various levels of interpretation of complex narratives. At the same time, Bruce's work indicates another cue system of which the accomplished reader should be aware. One might wish to assess the awareness and use of this system also. The general idea is that writers use the tools available to them to create cues which they feel will best help the reader generate the meaning which the writers intend to convey. In turn, the onus is also upon the reader to use these cues to infer (construct a model of) what the author intended. In a sense, accuracy becomes relative under these circumstances and, to an extent, one must tolerate a "band of interpretation reflecting varying degrees of reader-based and text-based processing" (Tierney & LaZansky, 1980). In this way accuracy is constrained by the reader's purpose for reading, his background knowledge, and the extent to which he is able to infer the author's intentions.

This author-reader interaction has also been conceived of as an implicit allowability contractual agreement between author and reader (Tierney & LaZansky, 1980). The agreement is similar to that suggested by Grice (1975) for oral communication, in which the speaker should be informative, sincere, relevant, and lucid. The written situation is somewhat different in that the reader cannot inform the writer of his progress in constructing meaning. However, in a sense this merely makes the writer's task more difficult, since he must make assumptions about the reader's knowledge and perspective in advance.

Kantor (1978) adds to this concept what he terms "considerateness." This describes the extent to which the author has lived up to his side of the agreement, in terms of his correct use of grammar and the flow of the discourse. That is, the author should generally make meaning construction as simple as possible for the reader.

Green (1979) has presented convincing evidence that newspapers represent a conflict of perceived intentions and goals. She argues that the journalists' beliefs about style, content, and format act together to obscure the structure of the story and its internal relationships, thus effectively blocking the journalists' own goals. This approach considers writing/ reading as one mode of communication, which in turn is one type of social interaction. Analysis thus requires us to consider the goals and beliefs of the interactants, and what the various text forms are intended to commmunicate (Bruce, in press).

Because the writer makes certain consistent assumptions about the reader and uses his own language and knowledge in consistent ways, familiarity with an author's style may aid reading comprehension. Children are sensitive to such stylistic differences at an early age (Green & Laff, 1980).

Both reader and writer have a complex task. Meaning is constructed rather than transferred; and both writer and reader play an active part in constructing meaning using the belief that small elements invoke larger, mutually understood schemata. Rosenblatt (1978) has claimed that our focus in the past has been on the writer or the text to the exclusion of the reader. Her focus is largely on the reader side of the reader/text/writer relationship. She suggests that readers are active in their interpretation of texts, attending not only to the referents of the presented symbols, but to their evoked images, feelings, attitudes, and ideas. The text acts as a blueprint to help the reader select and assemble what is being called forth. "A specific reader and a specific text at a specific time and place: change any of these, and there occurs a different circuit, a different event—a different poem" (p. 14). Rosenblatt thus suggests that we should think of a "literary work of art" as "...an event in time. It happens during a coming-together, a compenetration, of a reader and a text" (p. 12).

In summary, then, we must recognize the relationships between structure and content of text and the relationship between these as they exist on the printed page and as they or their effects exist in the head of the reader. Writers endeavor to present to readers such cues to their intended meaning as they deem appropriate. These they structure in such a way as to best represent what they wish to convey to readers. On the other hand, readers may read for purposes other than that for which the text was written and impose their own structures upon the text. This is an essential skill for readers to have. To choose to accept or ignore an author's structure, however, must be an active choice under given conditions and goals.

In terms of the assessment problem, the findings mentioned so far suggest that if we can manipulate different aspects of text structure and the explicitness of cues in the text, we may be able to examine which cues a given reader is or is not using and which structures are causing problems. Readers could then be alerted to such cue systems or structures. Thus, any proposed text classification system should classify along psychologically meaningful dimensions.

There is great variation within individuals across texts, and much of this variation is as yet unexplained. Observation of reader's performance on different types of texts should, therefore, provide much potentially diagnostic information which presently is not available. It is to be hoped that we are looking in the right places.

The Background Knowledge/Text Relationship

The social, linguistic, and cultural environments in which one grows up have their effects on test performance in numerous ways, some of which have only recently been uncovered. For example, children and adults may understand a question differently. The manner in which they represent the problem determines their understanding of it and their willingness and ability to answer it. A primary direction of study in this area has been toward examination of the effects of cultural differences.

Schema theory (Adams & Collins, 1977; Anderson, 1977; Rumelhart & Ortony, 1977) has highlighted the different effects of background knowledge in reading and stressed the need for culturally appropriate instructional reading materials both in terms of linguistic content and background knowledge. Cultural matching of early reading materials (and appropriate assessment) may help, but sooner or later evaluation in the "real world" will occur in the standard language. One could conclude that assessment would be more equitable if it were carried out with text matched to the learner's linguistic background. However, the standard for evaluation may not then be meaningful with respect to real-world tasks. On the other hand, evaluation which included both standard and dialectal American texts could perhaps be used to assess whether or not a linguistic mismatch was causing a reading problem.

A student might perform badly on a reading comprehension test simply because of a mismatch between his background knowledge and the nature of the text. Indeed, a study by Hall, Reder, and Cole (1975) indicates the likelihood of such an outcome by pointing out differences in free and probed recall of young Black children orally presented with text in either Black English Vernacular or Standard English. Such a mismatch can be quantitative or qualitative in nature.

Quantitative Differences

A quantitative mismatch refers to a lack of relevant world knowledge (for example, when a rural child reads a passage about city metro systems or a child who knows nothing about war reads a passage about the Civil War). Indeed, Johnston and Pearson (Note 7) demonstrated that a brief measure of background knowledge can predict comprehension performance on a given text better than standardized reading test scores can.

The source of difficulty in such a case is clear from the description of reading comprehension presented in the first section of this monograph. One generally cannot make appropriate inferences when they are required, and one cannot readily tie the new information in the text to knowledge structures. This comprehension may require the construction of new schemata.

Chi (1977) has shown that background knowledge (rather than age) has a considerable effect on short-term memory capacity. Extensive background knowledge allows one to store whole chunks of data in a single encoding, rather than storing each element separately, by simply pointing to an already possessed schema. This may have implications for assessment of reading comprehension. For example, perhaps lack of background knowledge could affect performance on multiple-choice questions more than on open-ended ones since there is a problem of keeping the stem in short-term memory while reading the alternatives. Perhaps when answering questions with the text not available for referral the problem is more acute than when the text is available.

Such quantitative differences in background knowledge could, in fact, readily be assessed, particularly given the methodology presented by Anderson and Freebody (1979; see the section on methodology). Armed with such knowledge, we might be able to make certain inferences about the causes of reading comprehension failure for individuals. These deficits might also show up in inference questions. However, without the information specifically on prior knowledge, one would be unable to conclude whether the failure was due to a lack of prior knowledge or failure to use available prior knowledge.

Vocabulary knowledge differences and why they produce discrepancies on standardized reading comprehension tests have received considerable attention (Anderson & Freebody, 1979; Hall & Tirre, 1979; Raphael, Freebody, Fritz, Myers, & Tirre, Note 8). These researchers have found extremely large differences in vocabulary between good and poor readers and across ethnic groups. If children have to expend much of their cognitive capacity identifying unfamiliar words in the test, less remains for building a model of meaning.

It is likely that lack of familiarity with structure creates problems just as does lack of familiarity with content. If narrative is the only type of material to which a reader is exposed, it seems unreasonable to expect him or her to be facile with other types of text. Familiarity with the structural cues allows the reader to find information more readily and know where inferences are required and what type they should be. A child who has never read a newspaper would have a good deal more trouble understanding newspaper items than a child who has had considerable exposure to newspaper items.

It is probable, however, that these differences are only the tip of the iceberg. The schematic knowledge and macro-structures themselves may be similar in extent but may differ considerably in their nature. For example, background knowledge for police may be similar quantitatively for innercity and suburban children but different qualitatively.

Qualitative Differences

The relationship between the text and prior knowledge can also be considered in terms of a qualitative mismatch between the text and the reader's background knowledge. This may pose a far more insidious problem—quite subtly causing the reader to build a completely inappropriate model of text meaning without becoming aware of the problem. It is not that inferences would not be made, but that inappropriate ones would be made. This problem could easily be self-compounding. Once the reader has begun to construct an inappropriate model, inappropriate inferences would be generated by virtue of the content of the growing model itself and the altered concept of "good form" so engendered.

Various contexts and instances of this type of mismatch are currently under scrutiny. For example, Hall (1977) has shown that with adults, social class and race—normally powerful predictors of reading comprehension performance—become less influential when content is made more job-relevant. However, even this does not completely eliminate the problem of racial differences. The developmental literature, too, indicates that children often can do a task if it is functional, even though they may seem unable to when it is not functional (Yendovitskaya, 1971).

Perhaps we need to actively test for this type of mismatch, rather like testing inferencing versus eliminating it from reading comprehension tests. Washington (1979) found that minority students and nonminority students differed primarily in their performance on scriptally implicit test items. These are items which require the use of the readers' background knowledge in combination with the text. If our sociocultural knowledge would allow us to do so, we might construct specific background knowledge items which would indicate the presence or absence of the background knowledge required for answering the scriptally implicit items. We may find that such information provides us with a context within which to interpret performance on other parts of the test.

Cultural differences in the nature and understanding of nonliteral language similarly present a problem, since most of these depend on social conventions of communicative interaction and congruence of attribute salience in order to have their effect (Ortony, 1979).

The problem may well be even deeper than this. Hall and his colleagues are developing a mismatch hypothesis which suggests not only that background knowledge differs across cultural groups, but also that strategies for acquisition of knowledge differ from group to group. The theory is that parents from different cultural groups reinforce different information-getting strategies. Thus, different predominant reasoning patterns would develop and hence, a different answer on a comprehension test may seem correct. For example, "main-pointness" may be a more white middleclass phenomenon than is "detail elaboration." Recent studies have hinted that innercity black children may find temporal material relatively easy to comprehend, but have trouble with "compare and contrast" material (Hall, personal communication).

The student's cultural vocabulary differences perhaps may be controlled by controlling the language in the test text. However, this will not alleviate the more general background knowledge problem. Several researchers (Royer & Cunningham,

1978; Tuinman, 1974; Washington, 1979) have suggested that making questions content-specific will solve many of the cultural problems. Unfortunately, this would probably require the use of only text explicit questions, and even these will often be affected by background knowledge (Johnston & Pearson, Note 7).

Asher (1978) found that children's interest in the text (highly related to prior knowledge) can have a considerable effect on children's performance on reading comprehension tasks. Given the material found in most reading comprehension tests, however, it is clear that this has not been seriously considered in test development. Indeed, with group tests one can never completely deal with this problem except, perhaps, in interpretation of test performance.

The implications of the findings for reading comprehension assessment seem to be as follows. There are three possible ways to deal with the effect of background knowledge in assessment:

1. carefully select texts and questions so as to eliminate those which might contain "biases";
2. assess in the language which is appropriate to the reader's subculture as well as in the standard language;
3. assess in various contents and language structures but include assessment which will discriminate between background-knowledge-induced problems and others.

Since the reader is likely to have to deal with a wide range of texts in the real world, assessment within a narrow range of texts for which there are minimal biasing effects of different prior knowledge seems of less interest than a more generalizable assessment. It does, however, seem unfair if such biased passages are included but not tagged as being such, as would happen in the case of the usual total scores which are used.

It is this writer's contention that we should be actively interested in examining background knowledge differences as sources of reading comprehension problems, rather than trying to avoid them. We are developing the technology for assessment (e.g. Anderson & Freebody, 1979) and the knowledge of specific areas which are indicative of such differences (Gearhart & Hall, 1979) which will enable us to produce potentially quite accurate measures of prior knowledge differences. Indeed, in informal assessments, teachers often ask this type of question already, although they have not been putting the information to full use in interpreting the remainder of the assessment because of a lack of understanding of the full import of the information.

The Task

It is extremely important that we should know exactly what we are asking the student to do when we set an assessment task. What factors other than those which we are interested in measuring will influence his performance? Research indicates that various reading comprehension assessment tasks can be considered in terms of the following factors:

1. production requirements;
2. memory and retrieval requirements;
3. reasoning requirements;
4. motivation;
5. purpose;
6. social setting and interaction;
7. expectation and perceived task demands;
8. test-wiseness.

Production Abilities

Production problems are difficulties in expression of information. For example, a child who is a very good reader may be poor at accessing information, particularly in an organized manner. Expressing ideas and organizing information from memory are skills which are not normally taught as part of reading, and skill in them may be quite independent of skill in reading comprehension.

Item types which are at the extreme on this dimension are free recall, which places a heavy demand on the students' oral or written production skills, and selection items (true/false or multiple choice) which place little demand on production skills. Other measures, such as short-answer questions and underlining, lie in between these two extremes.

These differences could cause a problem in interpretation of performance on certain test types. For example, children for whom writing is a considerable chore will doubtless have different criteria for what is worth writing down, from those for whom writing is simple. Production problems are almost certainly interrelated with retrieval, too, since organized expression may well act as a cue for recall of further information.

Memory and Retrieval

Selection items call upon memory in a different way from the open-ended items, and also require a different memory search strategy. Multiple-choice items can call on short-term memory for comparison of alternatives if the assessee uses certain strategies such as pairwise comparison of alternatives. Naturally there is a large difference in demands on memory if the source text is present or absent during question answering, though this difference may vary across item types.

Brown and Campione (1980) summarize the retrieval problem as follows:

> In short, we have a great deal of evidence that: a) people frequently store information that they are unable to retrieve; b) the presentation of appropriate retrieval environments leads to access of material previously 'forgotten'; c) different testing situations provide different retrieval environments, and therefore, assessments of the availability of knowledge varies as a function of retrieval support in the testing context; and d) the compatibility between encoding and retrieval contexts is vitally important as a determinant of the ability to access previously stored materials (Bransford, 1979; Norman & Bobrow, 1975; Tulvig, 1978). All these arguments concern the optimal conditions for making information in memory accessible when needed; it is not sufficient to simply store information, for unless it can be activated when needed it is of little use. (p. 9)

Reasoning

There are several ways in which the task may require reasoning on the part of the examinee. Multiple-choice items may require more or less reasoning depending on a) the strategy which the reader adopts to answer the alternatives and b) the plausibility of the distractors. Open-ended questions can require reasoning out which possibility the tester wants from the range of possible self-generated alternatives.

Reasoning also enters into the picture via "test-wiseness" such that part of the task of the student is to figure out the alternative cues for answers (e.g., information in the stems of earlier questions, or two equivalent distractors which must consequently both be incorrect). Indeed, the strategies used by students in answering multiple-choice questions are important determinants of the cognitive demands of the task facing them. Reasoning ability may also be more important for less coherent text.

Motivation

Work by Asher (1978) indicates that children's interest in text content may motivate their performance, and sheer motivation has been shown by Lahey, McNees, and Brown (1973) to have a considerable effect on the test performance of certain children. The motivation may also be affected by peer group pressure (Labov, 1972) and the children's cultural backgrounds (Clay, 1976).

There are motivational differences in the aspects of the text which readers find interesting. Stein and Glenn (1978) found that because first graders are more interested in the consequences of actions and fifth graders in the goals of characters, there are differences in what they consider to be the main point of certain stories.

Nicholls and others (e.g., Nicholls, 1979; Weiner, 1972) have shown many of the unmotivating effects of "learned helplessness" and it seems certain that this component of behavior will influence reading test performance, especially the extent to which children will apply systematic strategies and will persist with difficult tasks. It has also been pointed out by Keogh and Margolis (1976) that children with learning problems tend to be field-dependent and impulsive. Impulsiveness would be a particularly debilitating problem when dealing with multiple-choice tests. Nor should the problem of anxiety be overlooked. However, it appears that, in order to be effective the reduction of anxiety in test situations must be accompanied by treatment of deficient reading and study habits which interfere with test performance (Spielberger, Anton, & Bedell, 1976).

Purpose

The purpose for which people read a text tends to affect the kinds of information which they get from the text (McConkie, Rayner, & Wilson, 1973). Selection of reading strategies must be based on the reader's purposes for reading and these purposes can be controlled to some extent. They can even be manipulated implicity via the kinds of questions which are asked in successive passages or within the text (Reynolds & Anderson, 1980). Currently, those children who know the strategies which are most productive in reading to answer multiple-choice questions have a considerable advantage in reading comprehension tests. However, those children who use such strategies out of that specific context may find themselves at a disadvantage, since multiple-choice test items often tap details which would be considered quite irrelevant for many purposes.

The Social Setting and Interaction

Steffenson and Guthrie (1980) show that the language samples gained from questioning in a formal assessment/interview situation are qualitatively different from those gained from the same questions in a more meaningful situation. Harste and Burk (Note 9) found that when students read to them from a book and then gave them a free recall, the recall protocols were quite weak. However, when the children gave such a recall to a friend who had not read the passage, the recalls were quite full. Apparently, children are aware of the distinction between a socially productive and a contrived linguistic interchange.

Spiro (1975) found that with laboratory memory experiments subjects tended to differentiate stimulus materials to be remembered from other knowledge. That is, the subjects know that the information will probably be of no further use outside the experiment, so they concentrate on accurate verbatim recall instead of processing the input normally. Hence, they drastically reduce schematic integration. This is probably equally true of assessment situations.

Expectation and Perceived Task Demands

Part of the reader's task is to figure out exactly what the goal of the examiner is—what he or she wants to know or to hear. Consequently, readers probably respond to the same instructions in different ways. The effect of different variables is very much influenced by their perceived roles in the task structure. Consequently, instructions must be very clear and explicit, and even then the possibility of misinterpretation exists. Otto, Barrett and Koenke (1969) had children identify the main idea in four-sentence passages using the instructions, "Make up just one sentence in your own words that says what all the sentences tell you." Only 29% of their second graders could perform the task adequately. Danner (1976), however, found that instructions to find "the one thing that the sentences in the paragraph tell you about" enabled all of his second graders to get at least 66% of the main ideas. Danner also used orienting tasks to assist in providing task clarity. In these two examples, the experimenters intended a similar task but the children perceived different tasks, and rightly so. One task is asking for the *selection* of the topic while the other is asking for the *construction* of the topic.

Fredericksen (1975) used a repeated read-and-recall procedure in which subjects expected to be asked to recall the information in the text, or to apply it to a problem. Subjects' knowledge that they were expected to apply the information increased the amount of inferencing and integration evident in the recall.

The tester's control of the subjects' perceptions of task demands is small relative to the strength of the subjects' expectations based on their previous experiences with testing. However, one way around this problem is to first provide practice text and questions to establish the task demands. Reynolds and Anderson (1980) have shown that when readers are repeatedly faced with questions of a specific type (for example, technical term versus proper name), the readers spend more time and concentrate more on the relevant segments of text, and consequently perform better on those items. In any event, the task should not be left ambiguous, since the tester would then have no idea what strategies different readers used for different purposes, and in what context to interpret the results of the test.

Test-Wiseness

Readers differ in their test-wiseness, that is, in the extent of their knowledge of and ability to use different test-taking strategies and alternate information sources which are available in the assessment context (Sarnacki, 1979). Millman, Bishop, and Ebel (1965) provide an outline of test-wiseness principles which assist test-takers in their efforts. Furthermore, it has been shown that training examinees in these skills improves their performance on subsequent tests (Slakter, Koehler, & Hampton, 1970; Wahlstrom & Boersma, 1968).

In my discussion of assessment methodology, I will analyze certain assessment procedures in order to point out the information which they do and do not give to the assessor.

Summary

In this section, I have presented issues relating to the importance of the structure, content, and language of the text for a reader's comprehension of it, particularly in the context of his or her background knowledge. The extent and manner in which these factors influence a student's performance in various contexts has also been described in terms of the perceived and actual demands of the task. I have made an attempt to point out some of the interrelationships between these factors and specific characteristics of the reader and the task which can affect assessment outcomes.

This section on the factors which affect reading comprehension and its assessment has provided input for both what to assess and how to assess it. These implications are summarized and presented in the last chapter.

The next section addresses the issue of assessment methodology, and how some of the variables so far discussed influence it.

Chapter Three

Assessment Methodology

Introduction

Having achieved some consistent idea of what we are attempting to assess, and a good idea of which variables are likely to have an effect on an individual's performance, we are ready to consider how we might assess reading comprehension.

It would be very nice to have a procedure which is practical (in terms of fitting it to the constraints under which it is likely to be used) and measures what we want to measure— and *only* what we want it to measure. However, apart from the obvious problem that most reading comprehension processes are not directly observable, there are many constraints which affect the nature of reading comprehension assessment.

To begin this discussion of methodology, we must first understand the purpose of assessment.

Purposes of Assessment

Reading comprehension assessment is merely a more or less systematic sample of reading behavior which has been taken for the purpose of informing a decision or statement. This decision or statement can be very specific or rather general, and the level of specificity carries with it certain implications for the constraints which operate on the test, and the characteristics we desire in the test.

There are three main purposes of assessment, each with its own limitations and freedoms.

Administrative

Administrative assessment involves decisions about large-scale resource allocation, or general statements describing a given educational situation. It may involve investigating subgroups of the population to determine differential levels of public funding; or it may involve evaluating the results of a large-scale educational program to see if it merits continued support. While this sort of decision does not require information as precise as that required by diagnostic assessment, for example, decision-makers have often been accused of overlooking important differences among groups because of the global nature of the assessment.

The latitude which this assessment allows is that all students do not need to give the same sample of behavior. That is, one can use a very large test which has been divided up among students, only some of them having the same items. This is because decisions are made at the group level rather than at the individual level. This kind of assessment must be static, in that there can be no individual response-dependent adjustment of assessment methodology or difficulty. The test will be administered to students of a wide ability range and must have items of appropriate difficulty for the whole range.

Diagnostic

This type of assessment involves making instructional decisions at the individual level, such as selecting materials and teaching strategies. The requirement here is for specific information. However, for several reasons there is room for flexibility in diagnostic assessment.

First, since the assessment is not normative but ipsitive in nature, assessment can be individualized. That is, one student may have a completely different set of assessment materials than another student, since individual diagnosis does not require the range of difficulty which is necessary for group assessment. Secondly, the assessment can be dynamic, in that the technique, the level of difficulty, and the content can be response- and person-dependent. There is no requirement of standardization because if the domain is specified clearly enough, and the specific skills are assessed adequately, the test can be criterion-referenced. Nor is there a requirement to always examine a specified number and pattern of texts and tasks. Provided that the assessor knows what is being asked of the child and what it means in the context of a theory of cognitive functioning, the tasks, texts, and contexts can be varied so as to address the hypotheses which the assessor is shaping about the child's difficulties.

Selection and Classification

Tests for the purpose of selection and classification are generally group-administered, and uniform so that all students are compared on the same basis. Currently, the greatest limitation of these tests is that they must be suitable for a wide range of students, and yet each student must complete the whole test within the time limit. Another limitation is that the tests are not diagnostic or sensitive for the individual, yet individual decisions are made on the basis of the results. These problems severely affect the standard pencil and paper tests.

Although the above limitations generally prevail, this need not always be the case. For example, given complete enough information on students, and provided the domains are well enough specified, a scoring computer could conceivably be programed to skip tasks and segments of text which clearly would be too easy or too difficult for a particular student.

Constraints upon Assessment

Practical Concerns

Time is always a major constraint, and this is so for a number of reasons. Those working in the field, especially those in the classroom, have minimal amounts of time to devote to testing, especially individual testing. In any case, the examinee cannot give full attention for prolonged periods of time.

Generally, the longer the delay between reading a piece of information and testing it, the more difficult it is for the reader to access it; therefore, a different score interpretation is sometimes required. The more test items there are, the greater the chance of inter-item contamination. On the other hand, the longer a test, the more reliable it tends to be statistically. This presents a real problem for assessment, especially that which attempts to make broad generalizations about an individual's reading comprehension ability. Normally, a compromise is struck so that a brief, self-administering group test is given and an attempt made to gain maximal information from it by including in it a large number of short passages, each with a few questions.

The requirement of machine scoring of mass testing for administrative purposes also places severe limitations on test developers. For the present, at least, items are restricted to the selection type (true-false, multiple-choice, matching).

Item Sampling and Generalizability

Much sacrifice has been made in order to meet the above demands, but even more has been made to meet the demands of sampling theory. The idea in classical measurement theory is that one can generate an infinite number of test questions about a text passage, not all of which can be administered to a single examinee. Therefore the tester should administer a random selection of the questions. One of the results of current research is to demonstrate that, with reading at least, this is a very dubious approach (Anderson, Wardrop, Hively, Muller, Anderson, Hastings, & Frederiksen, 1978).

It is now very difficult to argue that a random sample of questions will give us effective information, since it is clear that certain information in the text is more important than other information, and that sorting one from the other is itself an important comprehension ability which cannot be taken for granted. As many have pointed out before, a systematic method of item development (preferably rule-governed) would be very useful. Even a rule-governed procedure for selecting items of specified types would be a great help. It seems that the prerequisites for this are beginning to accrue.

Such an approach might profit from the research on text structure as discussed above. If we can develop formalized ways of representing the information which is in the text, as well as the interrelationships between information segments, and the structural levels of importance, these may be used to select items in a more systematic manner. We could sample the kinds of information which we really would like to know about. If we can classify the type of information or relationship which an item is tapping, then we can begin to consider how the reader is handling various intratext relationships and perhaps generalize within these across texts or reading goals. This knowledge will also help us to define the domain to which one can generalize the outcome of a particular assessment device (Anderson et al., 1978).

The work done by van Dijk (1977) and Brown and Day (Note 4) on rule-governed summarizing presents a systematic method of stage-by-stage reduction of information to its most important elements. These rules potentially could be used to generate selections of questions at varying levels of importance. However, it must be conceded here that, as discussed above, importance is also governed by the perceived task demands and goals of the reader. Such a system would thus presuppose congruency of reader and author goals.

This system would also presuppose some sort of rational procedure for specific item generation and interpretation. Furthermore, as pointed out above, the passage from which the questions were derived can no longer be considered a random factor either, thus making generalization across texts difficult. This is especially so when the reader-text interaction is considered, at least in the individual case, where one cannot count on the text tapping a representative sample of the individual's background knowledge.

What may be required are more specific tests. One possible decision point which arises from the work of Hall (1977) is the functional aspect of the passage. That is, one should be concerned about choosing passages which have potential functional value for the reader, thereby ensuring attention and ecological validity, and minimizing bias. However, in doing this, one must be careful to assess possible increases in the passage independence of the items, since the more functional or interesting a text is for a reader, the more likely it is that the reader has some relevant background knowledge.

Passage Dependence

The whole problem with the item-sampling approach is that one does not really wish to know about the recall of random pieces of the text. The real interest lies in the degree of integration, inferencing, and general tying together of the textual information with information possessed.

With regard to assessing this latter aspect, it would be interesting to have some measure of what background knowledge the reader had before reading the text. Without this it is difficult to estimate his integration of new information with the old.

This argument leads me to reexamine the old issue of passage dependence of comprehension test items (Farr &

Tuinman, 1972; Hanna & Oaster, 1978; Pyrczak, 1975-1976; Tuinman, 1974). Test items are considered to be passage-independent if reading the passage makes no difference to performance on the item. Items which have been assessed as being passage-independent have been frowned upon for some time, yet without such items, we can have no idea of the extent to which individuals have integrated the new knowledge with their background knowledge, nor any idea of how much background knowledge they had in the first place.

It is here that the major cultural bias issues become apparent. Biased items are normally statistically identified and eliminated from tests without any idea of why they are biased. These items are most likely to be items which involve some inferencing (Washington, 1979). This is where background knowledge enters the picture. Cultural differences in background knowledge can cause different inferences to be made. Thus, any item whose answer is not explicitly stated in the text (and even some of these, since conceptual knowledge of single words can differ) is subject to possible bias due to differences in background knowledge (the source of the inference). Thus, these items tend to be passage-independent. To eliminate all such items would leave what have been called "low-level" questions.

One possible way of dealing with this problem is to include some of these passage-independent questions deliberately. By doing this, we could perhaps explicity tap the requisite background knowledge. This could allow us to begin to answer such important questions as why certain items are biased, and why certain individuals produced the pattern of responses they did. We can ask whether the reader had the requisite background knowledge and used it, or how knowledge differed from one subgroup to another.

Research has shown that passage-independent items measure something different from passage-dependent items (Tuinman, 1974) and, if properly designed, provide a good measure of background knowledge (Johnston & Pearson, Note 7). At issue, then, is a new approach to passage dependence, shifting from a statistical definition to a conceptual one.

The practicality of this possibility is given added weight by the observations of Anderson and Freebody (1979). These researchers, in noting that tests of vocabulary knowledge correlate very highly with tests of reading comprehension, suggest that a plausible explanation is that the word knowledge merely indicates a stronger prior knowledge of the area. If this is so, then a few well chosen (with respect to specific sociocultural differences), passage-independent vocabulary items could possibly tell us quite a bit about the reasons for certain aspects of an individual's (or group's) reading comprehension performance by indicating that the test was approached from a culturally different perspective.

Item Generation, Selection, and Classification

In the past there have been several attempts to formulate algorithms for the generation of reading comprehension questions (e.g., Bormuth, 1970). These algorithms were based on largely syntactic manipulations of the texts. The rationale behind attempts to derive question-generation algorithms is that in current tests of reading comprehension, the questions used are based upon the test developer's whims, and different developers will certainly produce different questions from the same text segment. Consequently, there is likely to be only limited agreement in the specific conclusions the test developers reach. Elimination of this capricious element is desirable (but not to the extent that it leads to stilted wording or ecologically invalid assessment, as many other attempts at increasing reliability have done).

It would be a very good situation if we had certain systematic and theoretically reasonable rules or algorithms by which one could generate appropriate questions for a given text-reader-task situation. Unfortunately, even attempts to generate such rules for specific texts have so far been unsuccessful. There has been, however, more success for post-hoc analyses which take the developed questions and analyze them with respect to certain of their characteristics.

Much information can be gained from a theoretical analysis of the relationship between the question asked and the source text. Lucas and McConkie (1980) have looked at questions in these terms and developed a system for classifying the questions. The system involves a propositional analysis of the text and a subsequent analysis of the source of information required to answer the question.

Pearson and colleagues (Pearson & Johnson, 1978; Raphael, Winograd, & Pearson, in press) have attacked the same problem from a different perspective. Their approach is to examine the relationship between the answer to a question and the text.

The two approaches overlap considerably. For example, one type of question relates to the ability to combine information which is explicitly stated in different parts of the text. Pearson and Johnston (1978) call these textually implicit questions. In general, it seems more difficult to combine information from two propositions which are further apart than from two that are close together. Similarly, it may be more difficult to combine the information in five propositions than that in two. Lucas and McConkie (1980) have included this information in their classification system. They refer to this type of question as "inferred" and code the numbers of the relevant propositions in the text (which has previously been propositionally analyzed).

Examining the processes involved in these questions, and even coding them, is complicated when information is repeated or is implicit in several places in the text. This type of question appears to tap "reasoning in reading"—essentially logical reasoning skills such as solving syllogisms (if A and B, then C)—and shows a close relationship to the work on problem solving presented in the first section of this report. It may well be that this type of skill is, as in problem-solving, readily diagnosable and readily taught.

On the other hand, these item-type descriptions may be applicable only when the reader has text and questions available at the same time. Once the information is stored in the head, little of the surface structure of the text remains. Thus it may be that these item-types lose some of their meaning once the text is no longer accessible. What is more likely to remain is a trace of the macrostructure of the text in the structure of the stored knowledge.

Perhaps these item classification approaches can be further developed in the light of the findings cited elsewhere in this book. For example, as yet, the question classification systems do not take into account such things as the staging of the information. Beck, McKeown, McCaslin, and Burkes (Note 10) have proposed that questions about narrative text should be based upon the narrative analysis (Omanson, 1979). This approach would allow a fairly objective classification of questions relative to their centrality to the main strand of the narrative. The centrality of information to the causal chain in narrative has been shown to have a strong effect on recall (Omanson, 1979), as has the staging of the information in expository material (Meyer, 1975) and whether the material is hierarchically or temporally organized (Thorndike, 1977). These factors may turn out to be more important determinants of performance than the components currently involved in the taxonomies. Research is needed in this area.

As a further example, the *main idea* type of question at first appears to be an extension of the *implied* type of question. However, the work of van Dijk (1977) and Brown and Day (Note 4) has shown that certain other explicit knowledge and skills can be utilized. Brown and Day have shown that children who are not good at summarizing text can be taught the skill by supplying them with knowledge of explicit summarizing strategies. Perhaps when the text is available, the "inferred" question assesses only a subset of the strategies involved in main-point finding.

As a further example, the long recognized "inference" or "scriptally implicit" question (Pearson & Johnson, 1978), if looked at in terms of Warren, Nicholas, and Trabasso's (1979) classification of inferences, may decompose into a series of more specific item types which are also more relevant to the manner in which the knowledge is stored after reading. Given Omanson, Warren, and Trabasso's (1978) finding that inference probes are the most sensitive indicators of reading comprehension, a carefully designed set of such items may give us quite detailed information about processing at various levels of reading comprehension, from the single word level to the discourse level.

Unfortunately, the work that has been done so far only deals with the stems of questions. There has been only limited application to the alternatives of the common multiple-choice item. This is a crucial next step if we are to continue to use these items, since the nature of the alternatives in part determines the cognitive demands of the item and, hence, the information which it yields.

Since the psychological reality of the systems of classification has not yet been established, much research is needed in this area. Clearly the approaches have important implications for the development of tests. For example, multiple-choice items could be based on Lucas and McConkie's or Pearson and Johnson's type of analysis, so that stems would have a systematic relationship to the text and to each other. The inclusion of staging or causal chain information would at the very least provide operational definitions of main-point and detail questions. Response alternatives could be based, for example, upon Spiro's (1980) analysis, so that production of different response options could be based on different, identifiable cognitive demands. Should such a procedure work, then diagnostic information could be gained from the test (subject to the reservations presented elsewhere in this book). The diagnostic value of the test would stem from patterns of responses on similar item types which would point to background knowledge or text cues which were or were not being used (appropriately or otherwise). Patterns of responses across similar types of alternatives might lead to a diagnosis of the kinds of cognitive difficulties which arose. The kinds of difficulties which might be picked up are similar to those outlined by Spiro (1980; see the first section of this monograph).

What one concludes from the foregoing discussion is that there are certain dimensions along which questions might be classified. The first is the source of the information which is required—text or background knowledge (or both) and possibly location in the text, especially in terms of its macrostructure. These dimensions may differ in their importance with the availablity of the text for reference when responding to questions. The second dimension concerns the cognitive demands which the question places upon the learner. Classification systems should also specify the relationship between the classification system and various reader purposes. In order to develop this dimension, there is still a need for research on the relationship between specific reader purposes and relevant reading strategies.

While it seems that we are still unable to produce effective algorithms, we are approaching the stage of being able to classify items and item clusters with respect to the information which they could yield. Thus we approach a position from which to select items which have a clear relationship to the structure of the text, the reader's prior knowledge, and the nature of the requisite cognitive processes. Knowing the characteristics of these item clusters, we should be able to generate tests which provide more, and more meaningful, information.

Reliability and Validity

There are two especially important aspects of validity in tests of reading comprehension. The first is concerned with the meaningfulness of the construct with which we are dealing. This has been a big problem for diagnostic tests, since the existence of the individual subskills being tested has been suspect. Our increasing understanding of the processes involved in reading comprehension will enable us to more rationally evaluate this aspect of the test validity.

The second aspect of validity refers to the degree to which our chosen assessment technique actually reflects ability in the specific skill which we claim it measures. To this end, some examples of the demand characteristics of various tests and test situations appear at the end of this section of the paper. Careful study of these areas is the road to a rational understanding of this aspect of validity.

Closer understanding of the relationship between reader and text, and of the nature of text itself, can be used to increase the validity of standardized tests, since we are beginning to know more about what processes we are measuring with certain texts and item types. Knowing the strengths and limitations of the different techniques may yet enable us to combine information from different measures to give us a highly valid measure of exactly what we wish to assess. Furthermore, since invalidity lies as much in the claims which we make about what we have measured as in the instrument itself, understanding the strengths and limitations of the instruments should help us to make more valid use of the tests.

Reliability is also a very important aspect of measurement. This refers to the consistency of the measure across different measurers and occasions. It has generally been argued that standardized tests have increased reliability but have achieved it at the expense of a certain amount of validity, especially ecological validity (the naturalness of the task). Informal tests, it is claimed, have the opposite failing: reliability is quite low (especially between scorers), but validity is higher. To an extent this is true, but progress is being made toward reducing the problem. For example, the development of text grammars has enabled more reliable and meaningful scoring of free-recall protocols: scoring which also seems to have some diagnostic validity. Here again, however, one is faced with the problem of deciding on the source of difficulty, i.e., input, retrieval, or expression.

Reliability should be looked at in terms of interpretation as well as scoring tests. This is the intersection of reliability and validity. Reliability is a prerequisite for validity. The context in which a test is administered, and certain demand characteristics of the text which are not integral to what we are attempting to measure, are extraneous sources of variability in test performance; thus the context and non-integral characteristics are threats to reliability. These factors may also invalidate an instrument which under certain circumstances may be quite valid. For example, the demands of the social situation in which assessment occurs can strongly influence the outcome of the assessment. This is clearly shown in the study by Steffenson and Guthrie (1980) in which the same task (the Peabody Picture Vocabulary Test) in different social contexts (test situation versus a real sorting problem) produced different results. The reasons for such differing results have been pointed out in the earlier section task analysis. Differing results, of course, would make the measure unreliable across these situations. Knowledge of these situational and demand characteristics will help us deal with this problem. For the present, however, there are problems with our current concepts of reliability and validity as they relate to tests of reading comprehension.

The concept of reliability, as Tuinman (1979) has pointed out, forces test makers to ask a large number of questions, many of which must test trivial information. This is so for four reasons:

1. The desire to generalize across different samples of text structure, content, and difficulty, has led test makers to include a number of text segments, which, because of time constraints, must necessarily be short.

2. Questions should be independent, and with a short passage, one is put in a position in which detail questions are very tempting.

3. Sometimes there is an attempt to use a number of questions of the same type in order to get reliability for each item type.
4. Items are selected on the basis of high discrimination indices, and the items which are best at discriminating are often those testing trivia (Tuinman, 1979).

One of the upshots of this set of constraints is to ensure that the brief passages are stilted, since the writer must cram information into each one so that a reasonable number of independent questions can be asked. Thus, the type of information which is often tested is knowledge of detail, which, for many reading purposes, is quite unimportant. We are consequently stuck with a measure of what children learn when they read for a specific, often dysfunctional, purpose, i.e., to answer multiple-choice questions. Worse still, children seem to have come to expect this of tests, so how can we effectively assess their performance when they are reading for other purposes?

It seems that in our efforts to gain reliability, we have sacrificed validity. This has resulted from a lack of understanding of how to evaluate the test other than statistically, and an attempt to answer in a single test the rather vast question, "How capable is this child, with respect to his peers (including all cultural subgroups), at reading comprehension in all types of text, and across all content and all situations?" Given the constraints on assessment, the question is one in which only administrators and parents would be interested. Since the parents in particular would be generally unaware of the limitations of the assessment, their interpretation of such numerical information would be more or less invalid, especially since their interpretation would generally be based on a single score. Rather than such mean performance information, the classroom teacher is more interested in individual differences which can aid in instructional decision making.

A line of research which is thus of particular interest concerns the "zone of proximal development" (Vygotsky, 1978; Brown & Ferrara, Note 11). This research is concerned with the inadequacy of current static assessments of children's IQ. The argument is that children with equally low IQs do not necessarily have the same learning potential, the difference becoming apparent when an adult or more able peer provides some assistance. It is the extent of improvement which occurs under some optimizing procedure which constitutes the zone of proximal development.

Such research has attempted to shift testing away from a standarized approach which attempts (but often fails) to hold context constant across examinees. The preferred direction is toward using the interaction between tester and examinee to find the conditions under which certain tasks can be performed, and how much of specified types of assistance is required for the child to succeed. In terms of reading comprehension assessment, this may amount to setting up different text and task situations which are apparently just beyond the reader's skill, and providing increasing amounts of information and instructional assistance. This has the potential of being considerably more diagnostic than other approaches, but its optimal use rests on the development of a set of texts and tasks with an associated sequence of prompts which have diagnostic value. For example, one could gradually reduce the demands upon production skills, organization, memory, and memory access by providing different tasks, and increasingly blatant prompts. Some of these prompts could be strategic in nature and others informational.

Thus, it seems neccessary for us to shift our perspective on reliability and validity, emphasizing the latter in the light of the factors which influence reading comprehension. Increased validity should incidentally improve the reliability of our interpretations in particular. This emphasis on validity will also force us into a different perspective on generalization, since it is clear that we cannot simply be random about text, or context selection and still ensure generality. It may be that we should be more interested in specifics than in generalities. Trying to reduce the effects of different factors may not be the way to do it either. For example, attempting to remove the effects of background knowledge by eliminating passage-independent questions simply will not work.

The Cognitive Demands/Information Content of Assessment Methods

As pointed out above, since reading comprehension is a mental activity, it is only available for indirect, second-hand scrutiny. We can never actually watch the mental operations, but must infer them from other sources of data. In making these inferences, we must be very clear about the grounds we have for doing so. In order to be so informed, we should understand (as clearly as our data and theory will allow) the actual demands and assumptions involved in our assessment techniques. For example, the process and product techniques are supported by different sets of assumptions.

Most assessment of reading comprehension to date has been of the product type and consists of a series of short passages (sometimes less than ten words) each followed by multiple-choice questions which bear some (often ill-defined) relationship to the preceding passage. These measures represent a very restricted view of reading comprehension, especially in their current state of development.

The object of much past development of reading comprehension assessment has been a single test which will tell us all we want to know. It is my contention that pursuing this objective in the current manner is futile, given the complexity of the reading task and the number of variables to be assessed and/or taken into account. I believe that a potentially more reasonable approach would be to refine and use the variety of approaches to measurement which we have available already, in the light of our knowledge of the skills and abilities involved in each, though we might want to add some supplementary approaches. By appropriately selecting combinations of these measures, we may gain a clearer picture of what and how a reader comprehends under a given set of circumstances. Research toward this goal will not be easy. Having first defined the elements of reading which we wish to assess, we must then characterize the nature of the outcomes of the different measures, and how these measures relate to and interact with the reading process. In this section I will attempt to lay the groundwork for such progress.

Product Measures

Free recall. The most straightforward assessment (in terms of initial preparation) of the result of the text-reader interaction is a free recall. However, it becomes clear at the outset that ease of preparation of the measure is inversely proportional to the ease of interpretation. While many researchers (and their assistants) will attest to the amount of time involved in scoring free recalls, such recalls may tell us something about the organization of the stored information. In combination with other measures, we can also make some inferences about the retrieval strategies which the reader uses. This, in turn, gives information about probable long-term recall of the newly-gained information.

Recent research has enabled scoring of recall protocols in fairly meaningful and consistent ways (Frederiksen, 1975; Mandler & Johnson, 1977; Stein & Nezworski, 1978; Fredericksen, Note 12; Turner & Greene, Note 13). For example, story grammars have allowed scoring of stories in terms of the presence or absence of the integral elements of the narrative structure. Summarization strategies such as those described by van Dijk (1977) and Brown and Day (Note 4) may ultimately allow us to examine objectively the extent to which the individual has been able to assimilate and reconstruct certain types of text. Patterns of intrusions, distortions, and omissions may provide valuable information on specific influences of the individual's background knowledge.

Although there is a lot that one can infer from and about the things that *are* recalled, one can say nothing about the comprehension or memory of what is *not* recalled. There are a number of possible reasons for failure to produce information in free recall. For example, production deficits are a problem. Alternatively, schema selection or access may be blocked or inappropriate. Or, as Harste and Burke (Note 9) point out, it may be that the reader simply misinterprets the task demands and, assuming (or knowing) that the tester has read the passage, gives only a cursory protocol.

What then are the cognitive demands of the free recall task? We must be fully aware of the large memory component which is invariably involved and the problems of retrieval. The reader must first clearly understand what is required in terms of the level of detail he or she is being asked to retain and reproduce (gist recall to complete recall including all pragmatic and possible inferences) and the degree to which recall should maintain the surface structure of the original passage. He or she must have understood and stored the information, and be able to retrieve it on demand. He or she must then decide on a point at which to start and a path through the information (e.g., start at the beginning and proceed to the end, recalling as much detail as possible, or give gist first, then return to the beginning and elaborate). A decision must also be made on a perspective from which to present the recall (Bower, 1978), and this may involve hypothesizing about the tester's perspective and working from there.

Production skills (oral or written) are also required, and production expertise differs across individuals. Unfortunately, reading comprehension skills and production skills are not perfectly correlated. Consquently, failure on a reading comprehension assessment task requiring production cannot be clearly attributed to production or comprehension skills separately. On top of this, the reader must be motivated to "play the game." Failure to meet one of these demands may cause similar recall protocols (in terms of the quantity and the pattern of the recall), so we must be wary of drawing unwarranted conclusions such as: less fluent readers remember less of the information, or the less fluent reader does not remember information from discourse in an organized manner (Marshall & Glock, 1978-1979) without gaining more information than is contained in free-recall protocols.

Probe questions. Probe questions following free recall locate more information which the reader has stored. Probes which present different perspectives are likely to produce different extra information (Anderson & Pichert, 1977), which is a factor that should be taken into account in free- and probed-recall assessment. Incidentally, such use of perspective as a retrieval strategy may well be worth teaching to students.

A problem with probes is that, to date at least, there is not a systematic method of generating probes which would be appropriate and which would be consistent across passages. Another problem is that even using probes does not exhaust what was learned from the text. A recognition test or sentence verification task (Royer & Cable, 1975) may tap even more information. The extent to which this is so may be useful information in itself since it may tend to indicate a retrieval problem rather than a storage or encoding problem.

One line of research currently being pursued (McConkie, personal communication) is a method of systematic probe generation. This involves analyzing the text and then locating the highest-level node not recalled in the free recall. This node is then used to generate the probe and, after further recall, the next highest node is located, and so on. It seems necessary to computerize this procedure, since one would require a minimum of delay between reading and free and probed recall.

The use of probes raises a further issue. Is there a qualitative difference in the comprehension evidenced by the information that was freely recalled and that which required probing, or is it merely a retrieval problem? For example, what of the reader who can answer any question on what he has read but if asked for a free recall has a great deal of difficulty producing an organized response? It certainly seems that retrieval and production problems are common enough and are correctable through instruction (Bransford, 1979; Brown & Day, Note 4).

The big drawbacks associated with the free recall plus probes are the following: a) For the teacher, it is very time consuming to administer and score, requires training and practice. b) For the administrator, scoring of large numbers of recalls poses horrendous problems. These problems would exist even if the protocols were written, which is ill-advised because the less capable students tend to write less well also, putting them at a great disadvantage. c) Generally, for younger and less able children especially, oral free recall is required. This must then be transcribed. If the most efficient probes are to be used, they must be individually and rapidly computed. Probes can, of course, be used without the preceding free recall. They then constitute open-ended questions or the stems of multiple-choice, true-false, sentence-verification, or other types of questions. d) There remains the problem of separating the effects of input, storage, and retrieval difficulties.

Open-ended questions supply different information from the free-recall information. While they are likely to tap more information, they do encourage further processing of the stored information. For example, inferences which a good reader might make while reading may not be made by a poor reader until the probe suggests the value of making such an inference. This complicates the interpretation of any probe-type question. One also runs the risk that information presented in one probe may affect performance on another. Research to clarify this area would be most welcome.

Assessment Methodology

For open-ended questions the production problem is still present, but to a lesser degree than with free-recall. However, somewhat different operations may be required by different probes, depending on the extent to which the original surface structure is represented in the probe. The surface structure is, in fact, a valuable piece of information, since individuals may perform differently on the probe depending on the extent to . which they stored (and were dependent on) the surface form of the text. However this type of information cannot be accessed without further research.

True-false questions. The next most straightforward type of question is the true-false question. These questions eliminate the production problem from the task demands but they suffer from certain other drawbacks. To begin with, a chance score is 50 per cent, which makes score interpretation rather awkward since the chance component is difficult to extract. Hence, one can never know why the reader gave the correct or incorrect response.

For the reader, there is a matching procedure required. If the surface structure of the questions is the same as that occurring in the passage, it may be a simple match. If not, then the reader must transform either his stored information or the information in the stem and attempt to match. If surface structure is similar to the original but the statement is false, two things are required: selection of meaning as being the more important cue, and a belief in one's own ability to understand. There may be an approach-approach conflict. The meaning of the stem seems wrong, but the surface structure may seem right. It is likely that a poor reader, who has had considerable experience of his own failure to comprehend, may well understand but decide to go with the surface structure indication since that is more compelling evidence to him than his dubious transformation.

The low signal-to-noise ratio seems to make true-false questions less useful as diagnostic tools; their strength lies in the breadth of material that can be sampled in a reasonable timespan. Their validity as a gross measure is supported by Anderson and Freebody (1979), who used them not to assess reading comprehension, but to estimate vocabulary size. They embedded nonwords to arrive at an estimate of the student's false-alarm rate. This allowed them to use a signal detection analysis to correct for guessing. These may well prove to be functional for administrative or descriptive types of assessment where one might want to make statements about the behavior of a broad sample of children over a broad sample of texts. However, one is still left with the problem of generating the stems for these items.

Multiple-choice questions. Most of the common reading comprehension tests use multiple-choice items. This item type is probably the most researched, most maligned, most difficult to construct, most abused, yet most functional of all items (when properly harnessed). It has the potential for reducing the problem which is evident in the true-false item, that of knowing why the respondent gave the answer.

The potential of the multiple-choice item for use and abuse is immense. The positive aspects have certainly not yet been fully realized because of the lack of theoretical and empirical reseach. Currently, the multiple-choice item serves only to allow mass objective scoring and to reduce the chance score from that of the true-false question. That is, we still get the same information (right versus wrong) as we got from the true-false item; there is just less noise. In fact, the multiple-choice item can probably give us much more than that. However, the extra payoff is dependent upon the development of a theory-based procedure for producing the alternatives. If selection of a specific alternative by a reader indicates a particular reading strategy or problem, then we can begin to look at patterns of similar responses, and the assessment can become more efficient. This legitimizes the questions, "Did the reader get it right for the right reason?" and "Why did he or she get it wrong?" because one could examine patterns of responses to correct and incorrect alternatives and make inferences about the strategies being used.

While the multiple-choice item still suffers from the problem which afflicts all forms of probed recall, that the cuing can induce processing which would not otherwise have occurred, this item type contains certain potential safeguards against the problem: by supplying a variety of alternatives which suggest different processing strategies, respondents could no longer find unequivocal incentives toward specific extra processing. One of the problems in reaching this goal is that, even if alternatives are theory generated, their empirical validation will not be easy.

The multiple-choice item in its common form probably involves a great variety of extra processing skills. There are specific strategies to be used. These need to be learned, and while they could be considered a type of reading comprehension, it is clearly not a type which we wish to assess in depth. These items require understanding of the stem, sometimes holding the stem in short-term memory, and using one of several possible strategies to evaluate the alternatives. Of course, different individuals will use different strategies, some of which will be maladaptive. For example, some readers do not read all the alternatives, but stop when they think they have the correct one.

These extra processing skills are clearly of a problem-solving nature. Some are not especially necessary for reading comprehension, and we would prefer that these did not enter into the assessment. On the other hand, we may be able to detect failures which are associated with a lack of these skills by using the information in the response patterns. Another way to avoid assessing the wrong skills may be to allow the reader to estimate the probability of correctness of each individual alternative (Pugh & Brunza, 1975; Johnston & Pearson, Note 7). This approach has three advantages. First, it guides the respondent through the steps of rational response to the multiple-choice question. Second, it does not force the individual to guess, although if a final answer must be given also, the tester would have information about the guessing behavior built into the rating scales. Third, the possibility of diagnostic patterns emerging is considerable, assuming theory-based stem and alternatives are used. This is so because the tester would have continous rather than dichotomous information about each alternative.

Another way of reducing failures due to inadequate skills is to go to some length to teach all children test-taking skills. This would still not completely eliminate the problem since, as usual, some learn better than others. Yet another alternative is to allow space on the test for the child to explain why an item might be considered ambiguous or have other problems.

Availability of Text. Reading comprehension tests may be administered in two different ways: with a passage available for reference as the questions are answered, or with it unavailable. While these are often used interchangeably, the difference in the cognitive demands of the two approaches is considerable. Again, if we recognize these specific differences, they may become less of a problem. Indeed, it may be possible to use the contrasting information sources to provide us with greater depth of insight into the processing differences among individuals. Assessment with the text absent clearly produces greater demands on long term memory, and cuing doubtless has a stronger function. Retrieval and organization skills are more important also. With the text present, more weight is placed on recall of approximate location of the information in the text, knowledge that one should look for it, search strategies, and logical reasoning skills. On an individual basis, the time taken and strategies used to locate information in text may also prove to be useful sources of information which can be readily observed. Summarizing text in text-present versus text-absent conditions represents the difference between the ability to summarize and the ability to store, retrieve, organize, and summarize information.

Process Measures

Process measures are more or less on-line assessments of what happens when one reads. Some of these measures contain certain amounts of product assessment in that they are dependent to some degree on memory components. Furthermore, while these measures are on-line, they are still indirect indices of comprehension processes but in a different way from the product measures. They do not necessarily indicate explicitly that the reader has comprehended, only that certain behaviors are occurring during reading. Their use rests upon a different set of assumptions from those underlying the product measures, and their use sometimes distorts the reading process by introducing an element which interacts with the ongoing process.

Miscues. One class of process measure involves oral reading. While this may or may not be representative of normal silent reading (there is currently no consensus about this), it can certainly tell us something about how readers comprehend text under certain circumstances. One of these on-line measures which some teachers already use is the miscue analysis, initiated by Goodman (1968). The rationale behind this lies in a conception of the reader as a rational cue user. In order to comprehend text, the reader's task is to make use of three cue systems: syntactic, semantic, and graphophonic. Goodman argues that by comparing a reader's oral production with the text we can make inferences about the progress of the reader's comprehension. For example, if the story is about a stallion and one child reads "station" and another reads "horse," one can infer certain differences in the state of their comprehension.

If reading comprehension is considered to be the systematic use of the cue systems to understand the intended meaning of an author, then Goodman's miscue analysis is a good basis for measuring certain dimensions of reading comprehension. It is, however, only a beginning since, as is indicated elsewhere in this volume, there are many more potential cue systems that the reader might use, such as cues indicating type of text (expository, narrative, legal document), cues indicating the task demands of the reading experience (social, personal, explicit, implicit), cues indicating the content area and depth (and hence the requisite extent of background knowledge).

The cloze task. The cloze task has been used to assess comprehension in many experimental studies and in classrooms, and as a benchmark for determining the readability of a text (the other side of the reading comprehension coin). While it is often used as a product measure, it is perhaps most informative when used as a process measure in oral reading. The task has its advantages. It is quick and very easy to construct in its basic form. One merely removes every *n*th word and studies what the reader does at the blanks. Unfortunately, it does not tell us why readers do what they do, and the measure is not without its problems. To begin with, performance is related to literary style. Hence, even if normally one would have relatively little difficulty with a passage such as part of King Lear, in the cloze situation considerable difficulty may be encountered. This is especially so if the common "strict criterion" is used. That is, if a response is only considered correct when it is an exact replacement of the original word. Such a system is probably often deceptive, at least for individual items, since one who understands well is quite likely to have available a number of synonyms. However, this may be less of a problem across many items.

The cloze task cannot be considered a normal reading task because often one must hold an empty slot in memory until one can locate information to fill it and construct a meaning for the segment. This places quite a demand on short-term memory, and there are search skills involved. On the other hand, if the characteristics of the text and the approximate level of prior knowledge for a given reader are known, one might be able to define situations under which specific problems arise. Remedial strategies could then be taught.

A useful modification to the cloze procedure which could allow the procedure to be much more informative involves deletion of specific categories of words in specific contexts rather than every nth word. Through careful selection of the type and environment of the words, one has more control over the nature of the task which the reader must perform in each case. This systematic knowledge of the syntactic, semantic, and graphophonic context at levels from word to discourse allows the assessor to put together information and make informed judgments of certain reader strengths and weaknesses.

There is still much to be learned about the cognitive demands of cloze tests, and research effort should be directed toward this end. For example, do different readers use different strategies to answer cloze questions? If they do, how do these strategies affect their responses? Perhaps an examination of eye movements during a cloze procedure in combination with data from a think-aloud study could answer such questions.

Eye movements. There is a growing body of literature on inferring from eye movements the strategies which individuals use in the act of reading. Currently, the necessary equipment is expensive and confined to laboratories. Nonetheless, this might not always be the case, and there is evidence that this type of study will help us to pinpoint individual differences in reading strategies (McConkie, Hogaboam, Wolverton, Zola, & Lucas, 1979). A record is made of what the eye does (as it scans the text) in terms of the location and duration of fixations, and time, speed, and acceleration of movements (saccades). The frequency and characteristics of regressions (look-backs) are also recorded. Armed with this information plus a detailed analysis of the characteristics of the text, one might infer some of the underlying cognitive processes by considering, for example, the types of text structure or content which were related to a greater number of regressions, or longer fixations, and so on. For example, if one staged certain information high in the text, one might expect longer fixations on that information, but only when the content was familiar. One might thus be able to infer the strategies which able and less able readers were using in certain text situations. Of course, if this type of data is combined with product measures, one might be able to make more inferences, and have better grounds for making them.

Dual task studies. Computers can be used to indicate whether readers are expending more or less effort on specific segments of text and, thus, whether or not they are attending to the structural characteristics of the text. The method is to have readers read passages whose characteristics are clearly specified, having them expose the text sentence by sentence on a screen. At various specific points in the text, a tone is sounded to which they must respond by pressing a button. The button-press latencies are related to the processing load at the time. The approach is based on the concept of channel capacity, and it seems to yield reliable information about concentration at different points in the text (Reynolds, Standiford, & Anderson, 1978). If this method can be refined somewhat, one could assess the extent to which, given a specific task, an individual is responsive to the textual indications of importance.

Self-controlled exposure procedures could also possibly be used to examine other processes in reading, such as the use of look-backs, especially when difficulties or errors are deliberately placed in the text. Another advantage of the computer is that such measurements could be taken in the context of a game situation, thus perhaps overcoming the problem of motivation difficulties normally inherent in testing procedures.

Metacognitive Measures

A considerable amount of research has recently been directed at examining what are called metacognitive skills (Baker & Brown, 1980; Brown, 1978). These are skills by which individuals monitor their own progress in tasks. The skills and strategies which readers use while reading need to be actively adjusted in the light of the state of the reader's comprehension relative to his goals. A second aspect of metacognition is awareness of the demands of the various tasks and the characteristics of the individual in relation to those demands.

This awareness of the strategies and when and where to use them is just as important an aspect of reading comprehension as the availability of the strategies themselves. The following assessment techniques require varying degrees of this awareness.

Self-corrections. Self-corrections (e.g., Clay, 1973) provide a potential source of information. They are closely related to miscues and result when readers monitor their own reading comprehension, as for instance when a child reads a word incorrectly and then returns to correct it several words later. The use of various cue systems can be inferred from the location and delay of the self-correction and its relationship to the original error. There are two main problems with the use of self-corrections as a sole source of information. First, they do not occur with high frequency under normal circumstances. Second, and more important, readers often find information that causes them to revise their earlier model, but they do not do so overtly. Nevertheless, as an adjunct and incidental source of information, self-corrections can be very informative.

Protocol analysis. Protocol analysis (e.g., Kavale & Schreiner, 1979; Olshavsky, 1976-77) is a clear example of an on-line measure which requires metacomprehension skills. This technique requires the reader not only to read aloud, but also to think or process aloud. The reader is expected to give a fairly full account of what occurs in his or her head while actually reading. This differs from a retrospective account and an introspective account in that it is more on-line. Of course, one must make certain bold and questionable assumptions about the ecological validity of such a task and the time delay between reading and interjecting comment; but given these assumptions, this technique also provides useful information on the comprehension process. For example, it can indicate how, when, or whether an individual uses certain information and how his model changes as he progresses through the text. Ericsson and Simon (1981) provide an excellent discussion of the validity of verbal report data. It seems that if the report relates to information which is still in short-term memory, then such data are quite acceptable.

The younger the children, however, the less likely they are to be able to perform such tasks, since young children have less access to this metacognitive knowledge than do older children. A certain amount of training is required before children can readily use this technique, but it is especially useful as they respond to questions, since it can help detect retrieval problems or test-taking skill problems. Such training as is required is far from a waste of time. It serves to provide children with access to their own thought processes, allowing self-monitoring.

Error-detection tasks. Another metacognitive task which has seen a great deal of recent experimental exposure is the use of children as critics who are asked to evaluate incomplete or faulty instructions and are supposed to say in what way the instructions are unclear or should be improved (Markman, 1979). This task requires the child to comprehend the instructions as far as possible, see that they are incomplete or erroneous and comment to that effect. This last demand is the big problem with this approach, since if the child does complete the task, one can say something about his or her comprehension and metacomprehension skills; but, if the child fails to mention the mistake, one is unable to say where the failure has occurred. It is quite likely that the error was noticed but was either ascribed to his failure or otherwise explained away (Winograd & Johnsotn, 1980). Nonetheless, the task has its uses, especially when a teacher has a good rapport with the children. It is most useful with instructions, and of very limited use with dialogue and other similar texts. This, of course, is reasonable, since the children have a right to expect instructions to make sense but are well aware that people need not tell the truth or be consistent.

This procedure in combination with eye movement or other on-line measurement might be a very effective way of observing the strategies which readers use to deal with structural or content disruptions, which amount to simulations of natural reading comprehension problems.

Confidence rating. Different variants of this task require examinees to place a value on the probability that responses or multiple-choice alternatives are correct. This approach has been debated as far back as 1929 (Greene, 1929). The principle motivations for its use have been its conceptual appeal; that it allows for the assessment of partial knowledge; and that, in combination with penalties for highly rated incorrect answers, it discourages guessing in multiple-choice tests (Echternacht, 1972).

More recently, however, interest in the metacognitive aspects of the method has increased (Anderson, Note 14). Not only can it assess the extent to which the examinees know that they know (or do not know), but with multiple-choice items it can also be used to examine guessing if equal ratings of different alternatives are allowed (Johnston & Pearson, Note 7). The approach may also have other benefits. For example, if individuals are required to rate each alternative in a multiple-choice question, they may be forced to process every alternative (which they may not normally do) and to process each one more deeply. One could argue, on the other hand, that the extra task demands interfere with, rather than assist, the examinee's performance. This remains to be studied.

Other metacognitive tasks. Collins, Brown, Morgan, and Brewer (1977) have used underlining or circling of key words or sentences to assess children's ability to select and study main ideas. They found that children below the seventh grade and educable retarded junior-high children do not generally perform such activities without being instructed to do so. When they are instructed to do so, only those children who have previously done so spontaneously seem able to underline important units. Others tend to underline unfamiliar, long, or random words. Circling key words is easier than underlining key idea units. Both, however, give evidence of the child's progress in mastering the skills of selecting important information. It might also be found useful to observe the child while he performs this task, especially if one had the child follow the words with his pencil. For example, pauses might indicate reprocessing, and lookbacks may also be evident. Note-taking is probably an even better indicator of reading comprehension. While it is conservative because of the production requirement, it nonetheless seems to give a good indication of the reader's comprehension, and hints at the processing strategies used.

Another possible assessment technique requires children to rate the relative importance of the idea units in the text. This is a readily scorable task and can provide information on the reader's understanding of the text. Brown and Smiley (1977) note that while third-, fifth-, and seventh-grade children's recall is highly related to relative importance (as rated by college students), there is differential ability across grades to explicitly rate the units. However, this may well be due to the memory demands of the task and may disappear if idea units were on cards and could be sorted into rank order of importance.

Brown and Day's (Note 4) work on summarizing skills has indicated further alternative outcome variables such as people's ability to summarize text. Even simpler components of such tasks, for example deleting the unimportant (or the redundant) information from a passage, could potentially give a reasonable indicator of reading comprehension.

The ultimate extension of the metacognitive approach to assessment is self-assessment. Collins, Brown, Morgan, and Brewer (1977) and Brown et al. (1980) have laid the groundwork for this, emphasizing the fact that children must be taught to monitor their own performance, by providing explicit instruction, modeling, and checklists.

Recently, this approach was put into practice by Pflaum and Pascarella (1980). They had children listen to tapes of miscues (initially someone else's, then their own) and sensitized them to the miscues which were being made. They then taught them to decide when they had made an important mistake or a less important mistake, and to take appropriate action. Thus the assessment technique became a self-assessment, and had payoffs in the children's improved performance in reading.

Summary

In this section I have examined a variety of aspects of assessment methodology. I have indicated some of the constraints which operate in reading comprehension assessment situations and how we might deal with them. A fair proportion of the problems might be solved by taking a broader perspective on reading comprehension, especially by going beyond standardized test scores. Standardized tests have generally restricted our thinking to product-type tests when we should be more concerned about the comprehension processes and metacomprehension.

Concern in assessment practice has been much more over reliability than validity. I have suggested that this situation be reversed. This involves a concern not only for more natural texts and tasks, but for using the contextual variability, rather than standardizing it, to come to a better understanding of the reader's capability. More careful analysis of the demands of the tasks which we impose upon the students should provide us with greater insight into why students fail on them. Generally, it is considered better to assess ability using a variety of tasks as sources of information, since each provides different information. Measurement of reading comprehension and awareness of reading comprehension are both functions of how performance on these tasks is measured.

An important part of our assessment procedure should be teaching the student to use the procedure for self-assessment. This has an important instructional function but should also increase the reliability and validity of our own future assessments of the students, since they will be familiar with the tasks.

Chapter Four

New Directions in
Reading Comprehension Assessment

Introduction

In describing the contributions of basic research to the assessment of reading comprehension, I have presented a picture of what reading comprehension is and what factors affect it. I have also pointed out how these factors affect the outcome of assessments of reading comprehension and the tension between what we require of tests and what they can give us. Tuinman (1979, p. 45) claims that ". . . once test constructors included inferential comprehension items in test batteries it naturally became increasingly impossible by any technique of statistical reduction to show anything but that reading was indeed reasoning." This book disputes that claim somewhat by pointing out the reasons for the high correlations between reading comprehension, vocabulary, and measures of general reasoning ability. Reading involves various specific reasoning skills. It also involves the use of already possessed background knowledge, which is probably what vocabulary tests assess. It is largely the background knowledge component which affects inferencing. However, over a number of different passages in different content areas, the general knowledge required will correlate increasingly highly with measures of intelligence.

Delineating some of the relevant reasoning skills is an important task. These are the *processes* of reading comprehension and an important challenge for us is to come up with ways in which we might tap these using measures available to the classroom teacher and, possibly, product-type, mass-administered measures. In this concluding section I shall deal with the following topics:

1. What can and should we assess?
2. How might we assess these aspects?
3. The characteristics and interpretation of reading comprehension tests.
4. Purposes of assessment.

What Can and Should We Assess?

This discussion has covered reading comprehension in terms of a reader's systematic use of various cue systems to produce a model of the author's intended meaning. Authors may or may not provide appropriate cues, and a reader may be reading a text for a purpose other than that intended by the author. It seems clear that text is not a random variable across which we can generalize at will, nor is reader purpose. We must know where the information is available to the reader and what cue systems are provided in the text so that we can assess whether or not the reader is aware of them, able to use them, and capable of being independent of them. Basic research is required to further isolate important textual and contextual variables which are involved and to describe their interrelationships.

In light of this, I have pointed out several cue systems which readers can use. I have also examined several cognitive reasoning strategies which readers might use to keep their comprehension abreast of their reading. There are two levels of strategies which can be described. The first set of strategies helps readers construct a model of the meaning of the text from the information available in the text. The second set requires readers to monitor their progress toward understanding the text, detecting lapses in comprehension, and initiating strategies to rectify the difficulties.

To assess comprehension, then, we might consider the following:

1. Awareness and use of the available cue systems in the text. The explicitness of the cue systems in the text affects how readers are able to deal with text. We should be interested in student ability to use cues

when they are present, and student ability to deal with the text when cues are not explicit. The degree of explicitness of cues represents the extent of the assumptions which the author has made about the reader. Some potential candidates for evaluation might be these:

    a. Text type, e.g., narrative versus expository versus rhyming poetry. We must await and encourage further development in the area of classification of text in order to do justice to this aspect, although macrostructures such as temporal form versus hierarchical form (Thorndike, 1977) or staging (Meyer, 1975) will probably play a role in this.

    b. Internal social-organizational aspects (Bruce, in press.)

    c. Author-reader relationships (Tierney & LaZansky, 1980).

    d. Perspective.

    e. Connectives.

2. Direct assessment of the reader's perception of the author's intentions and plans, especially when we get answers which do not match the expected ones.

3. Ability to override cue systems which do not correspond with the reader's purposes for reading, for example, when the text is persuasive and the reader's purpose is evaluative.

4. The nature of the text, especially in terms of its relationship to the background knowledge of the reader both quantitatively and qualitatively. We should directly assess such background knowledge differences to assist us in our diagnosis of problems.

5. Assessment, for diagnostic purposes, of whether dialect is causing a problem with reading.

6. Retrieval strategies, since comprehending without being able to access the information later is often of limited value.

7. Production skills which can be assessed separately from reading comprehension and taken into account in interpretation of production-type reading comprehension tests.

8. Information processing and use of prior knowledge. Is the student getting information from the text? Is it stored *and* integrated? That is, are the various logical and pragmatic inferences being made? Inferences may be examined according to the classification system presented by Warren, Nicholas, and Trabasso (1979).
9. Comprehension skills such as those suggested by Spiro (1980):
   a. schema selection;
   b. schema maintenance;
   c. schema instantiation and refinement.
10. Cognitive monitoring skills. Are the readers able to distinguish between when they do and do not comprehend? Do they have self-checking routines to evaluate this?
11. Knowledge of comprehension maintenance strategies, for example (from Collins & Smith, 1980):
    a. ignore and read on;
    b. suspend judgement;
    c. form a tentative hypothesis;
    d. reread the current sentence(s);
    e. reread the previous context;
    f. consult an expert source.
12. Assessment of knowledge of summarization rules and strategies (Brown & Day, Note 4).
13. Readers' awareness of when to use specific strategies; i.e., do they know the "triggering conditions" (Collins & Smith, 1980)? For example, given a reading purpose (e.g., reading for gist), knowing what to do when not understanding something (e.g., a single word) and the costs and benefits of strategies (e.g., skip the word and go on).
14. Assessment of children's understanding of the demands of various reading tasks. Such assessment would enable us to rectify potential sources of failure.

How Might We Assess These Aspects?

All assessment of reading comprehension is indirect, in that we cannot actually see the processes or get a pure measure of reading comprehension alone. By understanding the basic processes involved in the assessment tasks, we can understand what we do and do not know from our assessment, i.e., what inferences we can reasonably make about a child's performance. Thus we must take it as "given" that we can never have a perfect measure of the cognitive processes which we are investigating. We are bound to have some error or "noise" in our assessment. With this in mind, I will suggest some possible ways to assess the aspects which I deemed important in the previous section.

1. As the cue systems become more clearly defined, we will be able to manipulate them independently between and within texts in terms of their explicitness and appropriateness. Accurate assessment of readers' problems with various cue systems will necessitate comparable outcome measures across different texts; thus question-generation strategies will require more complete development before this type of reader information is fully realized. However, underlining specified cues or relationships may serve as an adequate measure of recognition.

2. In assessing ability to override cue systems, one could use the same measures as used to assess awareness, but provide the reader with a different purpose for reading. Merely asking students to read for a different purpose is generally not sufficient, they must be convinced that it is in their best interests to do so. This can be done by showing to and/or specifying for the student the task which is to follow reading. It can also probably be better accomplished by providing a practice task of the type to be required. Another effective alternative is to use questions embedded in the text. This technique tends to make readers adjust their purposes and, hence, their allocation of attention.

3. Understanding the effects of different text variables on readers' comprehension should show us how to select more optimally lucid texts. This will put us in an interesting dilemma as far as test construction is concerned. Should we assess reading comprehension using "perfect" passages or should we use moderately awkward but naturally occurring passages? Do we wish to know how a reader performs under optimal conditions or suboptimal conditions? Perhaps we will want both, since it seems unlikely that all literature will ever be optimally lucid. The contrast between performance on good

versus not-so-good text for an individual may well be instructive. Perhaps we will have to explicitly teach readers how to deal with writer inconsiderateness.

4. The passage dependency of items may possibly be used as a tool to separate out the effects of prior knowledge (such as potential cultural bias) from other comprehension problems, and to examine the extent of integration of textual information. Trabasso indicates that inference questions are the most powerful assessments of comprehension; however, in order to know whether a failure to make a specific inference was due to lack of ability to do so or lack of the requisite prior knowledge, it may be useful to ask specific passage-independent, but highly relevant, prior knowledge questions. These items could be used to detect not only the lack of appropriate prior knowledge, but also the presence of qualitatively different prior knowledge which could lead to incorrect answers on other items. This could possibly be done most efficiently using the true-false format of Anderson and Freebody (1980). On the other hand, the classroom teacher can, in informal assessment, simply ask relevant questions and judge the extent of background knowledge before or after asking the inference question.

5. To answer the question, "Is information which was comprehended retrievable?" one could assess comprehension immediately after reading, and reassess at a later date. Comparing performance on posttest questions when text is available versus when it is unavailable during question answering would also supply relevant information on this subject.

6. Looking for comprehension skill deficits of the type which Spiro (1980) addresses might be done in the following manner: Schema selection would be evident by providing a clear title for a relatively vague text (strong author assumptions), and comparing performance on this text with performance on a standard text. Schema maintenance could be assessed by constructing a text that has a context-setting section, then a long section that makes sense only in the perspective of the first section. Errors or points of possible misinterpretation could be embedded at various distances into the text. With or without embedded errors, oral reading of the text may indicate how comprehension is proceeding, as indicated by the

type of miscues occurring. Performance on these texts could be compared with performance on texts which did not make such demands.

7. To assess readers' skill at monitoring their own reading comprehension, one could build into the text systematic distortions (e.g., Markman, 1979); however, subsequently expecting the reader to voluntarily report finding the distortion is not a very reliable way of assessing error detection (Winograd & Johnston, 1980). A better way might be to combine this type of distortion (essentially a simulation of reader-generated comprehension failures) with eye movement data or self-controlled exposure times (computerized). Distortions could also be introduced at different levels of text organization. Another useful way of assessing comprehension monitoring is through the use of confidence ratings in conjunction with almost any product measure including, for example, ranking of idea units or rating multiple choice alternatives.

8. Knowledge of comprehension maintenance strategies could be assessed merely by asking readers what they do when certain situations arise, and asking them to take note of this when reading (i.e., introspection). One could even go so far as to construct text situations which would be likely to force readers to use these strategies. The think-aloud technique also could be used to get information on the use of these strategies. Getting readers to follow their reading with their finger or a pencil may give hints as to when they use certain of the strategies; eye movement data also would help detect certain strategies.

9. One could directly ask readers whether they know when to use various strategies (i.e., recognize the triggering conditions) and know the risks and payoffs of each. This approach would, however, only test whether they know the theory. To assess whether they actually practice the strategies, one probably would need to use a think-aloud approach since this is so highly dependent on the text, the task, and particularly on individuals, their skills, and prior knowledge. It can be assessed best in the one-to-one situation.

10. We must endeavor to make the assessment task meaningful and interesting. Unless we do this, we risk the children's failing because of their decision not to treat the new

information as "real," which leads to the failure to integrate it. Computers are particularly suited to this problem since there are already many commercially available games which require reading skills. Increasing the reading component and assessing the player's behavior following a clue, for example, may provide unobtrusive ecologically valid information on the player's reading comprehension.

11. A method for assessing the effects of dialect has been demonstrated by Steffensen, Reynolds, McClure, and Guthrie (1980). They used the fact that speakers of Black English Vernacular (BEV) do not use inflected forms of regular verbs for past and present tenses to show that, in situations in which the inflection is the only source of temporal information, BEV speakers have more difficulty than speakers of Standard English. The assessment instrument was a passage which the reader had to place in a time frame (yesterday, tomorrow).

12. The extent to which probed recall is better than free recall may indicate retrieval problems rather than comprehension or storage difficulties.

Many of the above techniques require one-to-one administration. For product measures, though there are alternatives, questions remain probably the prime source of information. They need to be more carefully constructed in order to refine the information. In any case, I advocate departure from the assumption that all things be kept equal in assessment; and I also advocate a greater concern with ways to use systematic variation in testing procedure as a source of additional information. This is in line with Vygotsky's (1978) notion of dynamic assessment, which essentially concentrates on locating the conditions under which readers can or cannot perform certain tasks, rather than simply whether they can or cannot perform them. For example, the number and type of hints required to prompt the correct response to a task is a continual and accurate indicator of the child's level of knowledge or skill.

Question Construction

Currently, test items are not generated in a particularly meaningful way. Perhaps this can be partially rectified in light of the studies presented in this volume. For example, an amalgamation of Pearson and Johnson's (1978) and Lucas and McConkie's (1980) classification systems, along with some additional changes, may produce a diagnostic classification system. Research indicates at least two dimensions along which items should be classified. One dimension is source of the information, i.e., whether it is derived from prior knowledge or from the text. An element which must be added to this dimension relates to the structural location of the information in the text in terms of causal chains or staging. The second dimension concerns the cognitive demands which the question places upon the learner. A further breakdown could be performed on the inferential questions in this dimension on the basis of, for example, Warren, Nicholas, and Trabasso's (1979) analysis of inferences. However, it remains to be seen whether these modifications will turn out to be effective. We must begin to develop multiple choice alternatives such that by systematic production of alternatives, comparison across items will yield more information per unit of test time. This will especially be the case if the alternatives carry their own individual meaning, each representing an attractive answer which would be attractive if the reader used a different specific processing strategy, a different cue system, or a (possibly culturally) different perspective. Unless we specify the task demands and goals for each question, the meaning of an incorrect answer, or even a correct answer, is unclear. When item development is based on meaningful skills, it is to be hoped that we will no longer select items on the basis of person discrimination (discrimination index) but rather on the basis of skill separation.

No question classification system includes items which are passage independent. Now that we know of the measurement problems caused by questions which draw on background knowledge and reasoning skills there are two opposing ways for us to respond. We could take the approach of Tuinman (1974), Royer and Cunningham (1978), and others who suggest removing items which are biased in these ways (Royer and Cunningham suggest that this need not be the case for predictive tests). This would involve selecting passages which dealt with generally familiar topics and eliminating from them items which were passage independent, or which involved some reasoning ability. Royer and Cunningham correctly point out that it is not possible to do either of these completely, but they contend that one should minimize these factors. It is this writer's contention that these two factors are involved in normal reading comprehension and that both are possible sources of comprehension problems.

Since we have the ability to know which items are tapping these areas, we should explicitly *use* the information which they give us rather than throw it away. Our behavior has been rather like throwing away a find of oil, thinking that it was just dirty black stuff. Indeed, we should actively attempt to refine questions so that they will give us the best possible data. To ignore these data is to pretend that reasoning and prior knowledge are not functional aspects of reading comprehension. This seems to have been a general problem since other assessment techniques have also been rejected for what they do not tell us while what they do tell us has been ignored. Perhaps, rather than throwing it away, we should have been using this valuable information by looking at the relationships between the "flawed" measures.

Characteristics and Interpretation of Tests

Venezky (1974) claims that comprehension measurement techniques should be tied to curriculum materials. This is only partially true. Currently, it can hardly be claimed that the design of curriculum materials for teaching reading comprehension is based on a theory of cognitive functioning, and this is what we are particularly concerned about when assessing reading comprehension. Indeed, such a concern may help direct us toward a curriculum which is more in tune with how children actually comprehend.

At all levels of assessment, an understanding of the processes which are to be assessed is crucial. It is difficult to measure something of which we do not have a clear concept. It is through such a theoretical framework that we can come to understand individual differences and how to respond to those differences which we record. Such knowledge of text and of text processing must be coupled with knowledge of the demands of our assessment tasks so that we know exactly what we have asked the child to do. Thus we might gain knowledge of the various possible sources of error. This also allows us to minimize the number of error sources by ensuring that the child's understanding of the task is the same as ours, and that the situation is appropriate and motivating. Indeed, we should directly teach him the skills and strategies required for taking our tests.

The most important function of recent research in reading comprehension, with respect to its assessment, is largely as metaknowledge. That is, it allows us to become aware of what we do and do not know when we have assessed a child's reading comprehension, and points out what we could know. We should now be able to make improvements in both reliability and validity, but especially in validity. To date, reliability has been acceptable but validity has been somewhat less acceptable in terms of the reality of the subskills under assessment. This has been so because of the inadequacy of the tests to assess them effectively, and because of the lack of ecological validity. I wish to de-emphasize reliability (without losing it) and emphasize validity.

Both reliability and validity must be looked at in terms of the decisions which result from our assessments. Greater understanding of strengths and weaknesses of procedures can help increase both aspects of our decision-making. Validity can be increased by better understanding of a) what is being measured, b) how to measure it, and c) what factors influence performance and, hence, must be taken into account when interpreting performance. As a result of increasing the validity of the tests there should be an associated increase in reliability because of a) clearer specification of parallel forms and b) greater understanding of, and ability to control for, the effects of extraneous factors. These factors can potentially invalidate an instrument which, under certain circumstances, is quite valid. For example, the demands of the social situation in which assessment occurs can strongly influence the outcome of the assessment (Steffensen & Guthrie, 1980). It is this writer's opinion that informed use of measurement devices is the key to ensuring test validity, since validity can be built into tests only to a certain degree. Invalidity lies as much in the claims which we make about what we have measured as in the instrument itself. In this light then, the following general cautions and considerations are presented:

1. Current reading comprehension assessment practices are unsatisfactory partly because of the constraints

placed upon them. The problems stem not only from practical constraints but from conflicting theoretical concerns as well.

2. We cannot see cognitive processes. Cognitive and developmental psychology are helping solve this problem by analyzing various cognitive tasks experimentally and by showing us when the cognitive strategies are evident or at least close to the surface—for example, the think-aloud and error-detection paradigms. Teaching readers how to be introspective, and what things to be aware of may also later assist us through self-report.

3. Item selection and construction can and must become more systematic. The information available from assessment will thus become more useful.

4. Using more questions makes for greater reliability but more interitem correlation also. Unfortunately, using more items also means increased time demands and often a decrease in attention. The intent here is to increase the efficiency of testing by making explicitly clear what we are testing and by using tasks with known properties (both similar and different) in which responses provide maximum information.

5. The assessment task should be carefully analyzed and made quite explicit so that it is very clear to both assessor and assessee. Specification of the task should be such that one can understand the meaning of a "wrong" answer as well as a "right" answer. Knowing exactly what abilities we are assessing when we use a test enables us to increase the validity of the decisions and statements which we make as a result of the assessment.

6. Knowing what factors can affect our assessments can increase the reliability of our findings by allowing us to account for more of the variability in our findings thus increasing the agreement on interpretation.

7. It may be that children look on reading comprehension assessment as a special task and treat any information gained through such required reading as "different" and deliberately reduce schematic integration.

8. By systematically varying the tasks which the reader must perform, we may be able to assess which aspects of the reading task may be causing problems for the reader.

9. These tasks should be highly related to normal societal demands on reading performance.

10. We must carefully consider the social aspects of our assessment both in terms of the effects of the testing situation

on the perceived task, and in terms of the social import of the assessment to the individual.

11. Assessment texts should include texts which are complete enough to have macrostructures.

12. The order in which a reader reads a series of texts affects the comprehension of each. Text constructors must consider this variable in compiling tests, just as they must consider primacy and recency effects of information occurrence in each text.

13. The assumption underlying the more recent analysis of texts is that the text is a communicative device. Someone has produced it in an effort to convey meaning to someone else. This does not seem like a big assumption, but in reading various passages in reading comprehension tests, it becomes clear that this assumption is sometimes violated.

14. People approach different types of text differently. That is, one might not normally read an expository piece on a scientific topic in the same way as, say, a Shakespearean sonnet, or *True Romances*. Certain goals are more likely for certain types of text. Indeed, the motivation for reading at all (as well as for reading with different strategies) may be controlled by the type, and certainly the relevance, of the text. A youngster whose chief concern is to learn how to fix bikes may well be able to perform adequately on service manual comprehension tasks but fail on poetic or narrative forms. These should not be muddled in our assessment by giving a global test score on a nonspecific text type with a nonspecific purpose.

15. Assessment texts should be motivating. If they are not, this should be taken into account as a possible cause for failure when interpreting the test. Texts should include variation in those factors which we think may affect the individual's performance, such as dialect and background knowledge. These factors should also be directly assessed through the questions.

16. It is possible to have situations in which a reader may have used all the appropriate strategies, but have developed an inappropriate model of the author's meaning because of deficient or different background knowledge. We should begin to take into account in our assessments the possibility of alternative plausible interpretations of text. This

might be done through the use of free recalls, or by allowing comments on multiple choice questions, which could indicate to an assessor the reasoning underlying an answer.

17. A child's readiness to respond to a question is determined by a number of variables besides his or her understanding of the question.

18. Probably the best way to assess reading comprehension is to use two or three different types of measure, each based on different assumptions and with different sources of error. This gives firmer grounds for such inferences as one wishes to make and allows a greater variety of inferences.

We shall now consider the implications in terms of the distinction made earlier between the three levels of decision-making: administrative, diagnostic, and selection.

Administrative Assessment

From the earlier discussion of text and task variables, it seems clear that accounting for all of them in a single test which also requires a range of difficulty and passages of reasonable length, and has a fairly strict time limit, would be difficult to say the least. However, since the decisions are not at the level of the individual pupil (or test paper) it is not necessary for all children to take the same test. The best way to deal with this is to devise a test using all the parameters, then use multiple matrix sampling techniques to produce a series of separate test booklets containing parts of the test. Thus, several pupils take the test. Selection of items on different forms can be made in a systematic way so that each child gets items with certain relationships among them, and certain items which other children also get. Thus, very sensitive program evaluation could be done, and more meaningful decisions could be made. One would have, in a sense, program diagnostic information.

Diagnostic Assessment

The major thrust must be toward individual, diagnostic assessment in which the aim is to specify not merely that the child can or cannot perform a particular task, but to specify the *conditions under which* the child can or cannot do it. In order to assess in this manner, the assessor first needs to have a theory with which to generate testable hypotheses about the reasons for the reader's performance. Second, the assessor also needs to know the capabilities and limitations of the various assessment techniques. Third, he or she must be well aware of the factors which represent the conditions under which comprehension occurred. Awareness of each of these factors can make the teacher a more sensitive observer of behavior and thus, ultimately, a continuous, unobtrusive assessor. At that point, instruction and assessment effectively become one. The assessment is a matter of locating the "leading edge" of a child's performance and defining the generality of his or her performance. The assessment requires presenting the child with tasks in the optimal challenge range and examining how much and what type of extra prompting or other assistance is needed to enable him or her to deal successfully with the task.

I have also suggested that if our assessment procedures are reasonable, then they should be taught to the child, since not only will that reduce the extraneous information which we get in later assessments, but it will allow the child to monitor his or her own reading comprehension. This type of self-monitoring instruction is a must. We should make completely clear the assessment demands of our instruction and give the child practice at using the techniques.

We should recognize the importance in our assessment procedures of such variables as retrieval strategies, and teach them. Rather than being concerned about them as potentially confusing byproducts, we would do well to look more carefully at them and their role in reading comprehension. Perhaps what we require is a systematic way of selecting assessment procedures for given situations, readers, tasks, and texts.

Selection Assessment

As explained previously, this type of test generally needs to be group administered, but the decisions are to be made at the individual level. This presents an awkward trade-off situation in that we need much information which we cannot get because we are forced to use the time ineffectively. Since the test must cater to a range of ability, pupils spend a good part of their test time on materials that are inappropriate and tell us little. While we can make the assessment somewhat more efficient by using systematic item and alternative selection, we still cannot eliminate the problem.

I contend that these tests may be used for initial grouping practices in the classrooms and schools, but only with great caution. If they are used with a good understanding of their problems and inaccuracies, they may be functional as initial gross screening devices. However, we believe that currently too much emphasis is placed on the results of such tests (for example, Title I placement) and that teachers should be far more wary of the scores and more accepting of their own analyses. I am hopeful that the training of teachers will begin to include more comprehensive work on the skills teachers require for the dynamic interactive type of assessment discussed earlier.

Computers may provide a partial solution to certain problems associated with motivation, efficiency, and time constraints. By using branching programs which adjust text, item type, and difficulty on the basis of initial item performance, more efficiency could be achieved. Thus, some of the benefits of individualized assessment could be gained without additional time investment from the teacher. The motivational aspect may be dealt with by building these into computer games which pupils would play for amusement and which would incidentally require certain reading skills. Assessment could be continually adjusted, assessing comprehension via the child's responses, such as the number of hints required (each costing a quantity of treasure) to gain certain crucial information from a segment of text. As the initial cost of the necessary equipment continues to drop, such developments will certainly prove very useful.

In conclusion, an attempt has been made in this volume to provide what amounts to assessment metaknowledge such that readers, having assessed students' reading comprehension, have a better idea of what the students can and cannot do and how they might go about finding out more.

Reference Notes

1. Derrick, D. *Three aspects of reading comprehension as measured by tests of different lengths* (Research Bulletin 53-8). Princeton, New Jersey: Educational Testing Service, 1953.
2. Pace, A. J. *The influence of world knowledge in children's comprehension of short narrative passages.* Paper presented at the annual meeting of the American Educational Research Association, Toronto, March 1978.
3. Wilensky, R. *Understanding goal-based stories* (Research Report No. 140). New Haven, Connecticut: Yale University, Department of Computer Science, 1978.

4. Brown, A. L., & Day, J. D. *Developmental trends in the use of summarization rules.* Paper presented at the meeting of the American Educational Research Association, Boston, 1980.

5. Stein, N. L., & Glenn, C. G. *The role of structural variation in children's recall of simple stories.* Paper presented at the meeting of the Society for Research in Child Development, New Orleans, 1977.

6. Adams, M., Bruce, B., Cohen, P., Collins, A., Gentner, D., Rubin, A., Smith, E., Starr, B., Starr, K., & Steinberg, C. *Progress Report 3 on the BBN Group of the Center for the Study of Reading* (BBN Report No. 4461). Cambridge, Massachusetts: Bolt Beranek and Newman, July 1980.

7. Johnston, P. H., & Pearson, P. D. *Explicitness of connectives and content familiarity as determinants of reading comprehension.* Paper presented at the annual meeting of the National Reading Conference, San Diego, December 1980.

8. Raphael, T. E., Freebody, P., Fritz, M., Myers, A. C., & Tirre, W. C. *Contrasting the effects of some text variables on comprehension and ratings of comprehensibility.* Paper presented at the annual meeting of the American Educational Research Association, Boston, 1980.

9. Harste, J., & Burke, C. *Reexamining retellings as comprehension devices.* Paper presented at the National Reading Conference, San Antonio, December 1979.

10. Beck, I. L., McKeown, M. G., McCaslin, E. S., & Burkes, A. M. *Instructional dimensions that may affect reading comprehension: Examples from two commercial programs* (Tech. Rep.). Pittsburgh: University of Pittsburgh, Learning Research and Development Center, 1979.

11. Brown, A. L., & Ferrara, R. A. *Diagnosing zones of potential development: An alternative to standardized testing?* (Tech. Rep. to appear). Urbana: University of Illinois, Center for the Study of Reading, in preparation.

12. Frederiksen, C. H. *Inference structure and the structure of children's discourse.* Paper presented at the Symposium on the Development of Discourse Processing Skills, Society for Research in Child Development, New Orleans, 1977.

13. Turner, A., & Greene, E. *The construction and use of a propositional text base.* Report from the Institute for the Study of Intellectual Behavior, University of Colorado, April 1977.

14. Anderson, R. I. *Confidence testing: A means to assess a metacognitive component of test item responses.* Unpublished manuscript, University of Illinois, 1980.

References

Adams, M., & Bruce, B. *Background knowledge and reading comprehension* (Reading Education Rep. No. 13). Urbana: University of Illinois, Center for the Study of Reading, January 1980. (ED 181 431)

Adams, M.J., & Collins, A. *A schema-theoretic view of reading comprehension* (Tech. Rep. No. 32). Urbana: University of Illinois, Center for the Study of Reading, April 1977. (ED 142 971)

Aiken, E.G., Thomas, G.S., & Shennum, W.A. Memory for a lecture: Effects of notes, lecture rate and information density. *Journal of Educational Psychology*, 1975, *67*, 439-444.

Anderson, R. C. *Schema-directed processes in language comprehension* (Tech. Rep. No. 50). Urbana: University of Illinois, Center for the Study of Reading, July 1977. (ED 142 977)

Anderson, R. C., & Freebody, P. *Vocabulary knowledge* (Tech. Rep. No. 136). Urbana: University of Illinois, Center for the Study of Reading, August 1979. (ED 177 480)

Anderson, R. C., & Pichert, J. W. *Recall of previously unrecallable information following a shift in perspective* (Tech. Rep. No. 41). Urbana: University of Illinois, Center for the Study of Reading, April 1977. (ED 142 974)

Anderson, R. C., Spiro, R. J., & Anderson, M. C. *Schemata as scaffolding for the representation of information in connected discourse* (Tech. Rep. No. 24). Urbana: University of Illinois, Center for the Study of Reading, March 1977. (ED 136 236)

Anderson, T. H., Wardrop, J. L., Hively, W., Muller, K. E., Anderson, R. I., Hastings, C. N., & Fredericksen, J. *Development and trial of a model for developing domain referenced tests of reading comprehension* (Tech. Rep. No. 86). Urbana: University of Illinois, Center for the Study of Reading, May 1978. (ED 157 036)

Andrich, D., & Godfrey, J. R. Hierarchies in the skills of Davis' Reading Comprehension Test Form D: An empirical investigation using a latent trait model. *Reading Research Quarterly*, 1978, *14*, 183-200.

Asher, S. R. *Influence of topic interest on black and white children's reading comprehension* (Tech. Rep. No. 99). Urbana: University of Illinois, Center for the Study of Reading, July 1978. (ED 159 661)

Baker, L. *Comprehension monitoring: Identifying and coping with text confusions* (Tech. Rep. No. 145). Urbana: University of Illinois, Center for the Study of Reading, September 1979. (ED 177 525)

Baker, L., & Brown, A. L. *Metacognitive skills and reading* (Tech. Rep. No. 188). Urbana: University of Illinois, Center for the Study of Reading, November 1980.

Baker, L., & Stein, N. L. *The development of prose comprehension skills* (Tech. Rep. No. 102). Urbana: University of Illinois, Center for the Study of Reading, September 1978. (ED 159 663)

Bateman, D., Frandsen, K., & Dedmon, D. Dimensions of "Lecture comprehension": A factor analysis of listening test items. *Journal of Communication*, 1964, *14*, 183-189.

Bormuth, J. R. *On the theory of achievement test items.* Chicago: University of Chicago Press, 1970.

Bower, G. H. Experiments on story comprehension and recall. *Discourse Processes*, 1978, *l*, 211-231.

Bransford, J. D. *Human cognition: Learning, understanding and remembering.* Belmont, California: Wadsworth, 1979.

Bransford, J. D., & Johnson, M. K. Contextual prereqisites for understanding: Some investigations of comprehension and recall. *Journal of Verbal Learning and Verbal Behavior*, 1972, *11*, 717-726.

Bransford, J. D., & Johnson, M. K. Consideration of some problems of comprehension. In W. G. Chase (Ed.), *Visual information processing*. New York: Academic Press, 1973.

Brown, A. L. The development of memory: Knowing, knowing about knowing, and knowing how to know. In H. W. Reese (Ed.), *Advances in child development and behavior* (Vol. 10). New York: Academic Press, 1975.

Brown, A. L. Knowing when, where, and how to remember: A problem of metacognition. In R. Glaser (Ed.), *Advances in instructional psychology*. Hillsdale, New Jersey: Erlbaum, 1978.

Brown, A. L., & Campione, J. C. *Inducing flexible thinking: The problem of access* (Tech. Rep. No. 156). Urbana: University of Illinois, Center for the Study of Reading, January 1980. (ED 181 428)

Brown, A. L., Campione, J. C., & Day, J. *Learning to learn* (Tech. Rep. 189). Urbana: University of Illinois, Center for the Study of Reading, November 1980.

Brown, A. L., & French, L. A. Construction and reconstruction of logical sequence using causes or consequences as the point of departure. *Child Development*, 1976, *47*, 930-940.

Brown, A. L., & Murphy, M. D. Reconstruction of arbitrary versus logical sequences by preschool children. *Journal of Experimental Child Psychology*, 1975, *20*, 307-326.

Brown, A. L., & Smiley, S. S. *The development of strategies for studying prose passages* (Tech. Rep. No. 66). Urbana: University of Illinois, Center for the Study of Reading, October 1977. (ED 145 371)

Bruce, B. C. *A social interaction model of reading* (Tech. Rep. to appear). Urbana: University of Illinois, Center for the Study of Reading, in press.

Canney, G., & Winograd, P. *Schemata for reading and reading comprehension performance* (Tech. Rep. No. 120). Urbana: University of Illinois, Center for the Study of Reading, April 1979. (ED 169 520)

Carroll, J. B. *Learning from verbal discourse in educational media: A review of the literature*, 1971. (ED 058 771)

Chi, M. T. H. Short-term memory limitations in children: Capacity or processing deficits? *Memory and Cognition*, 1976, *4*, 559-572.

Chi, M.T.H. Age differences in memory span. *Journal of Experimental Child Psychology*, 1977, *23*, 266-281.

Chi, M. T. H. Knowledge development and memory performance. To appear in M. Friedman, J. P. Das, & N. O'Connor (Eds.), *Intelligence and learning*. New York: Plenum Press, in press.

Clay, M. M. *Reading: The patterning of complex behavior*. Auckland, New Zealand: Heinemann Educational Books, 1973.

Clay, M. M. Early childhood and cultural diversity. *Reading Teacher*, 1976, *29*, 333-342.

Clements, P. *The effects of staging on recall from prose*. Unpublished doctoral dissertation, Cornell University, 1976.

Coleman, E. B. Developing a technology of written instruction: Some determinants of the complexity of prose. In E. Rothkopf & P. Johnson (Eds.), *Verbal learning research and the technology of written instruction*. New York: Columbia University Teachers College Press, 1971.

Collins, A., Brown, J. S., & Larkin, K. M. *Inference in text understanding* (Tech. Rep. No. 40). Urbana: University of Illinois, Center for the Study of Reading, December 1977. (ED 145 404)

Collins, A., Brown, A. L., Morgan, J. L., & Brewer, W. F. *The analysis of reading tasks and texts* (Tech. Rep. No. 43). Urbana: University of Illinois, Center for the Study of Reading, April 1977. (ED 145 404)

Collins, A., & Smith, E. *Teaching the process of reading comprehension* (Tech. Rep. No. 182). Urbana: University of Illinois, Center for the Study of Reading, September 1980.

Danner, F. W. Children's understanding of intersentence organization in the recall of short descriptive passages. *Journal of Educational Psychology*, 1976, *68*, 174-183.

Davis, F. B. Fundamental factors of comprehension of reading. *Psychometrika*, 1944, *9*, 185-197.

Davis, F. B. Research in comprehension in reading. *Reading Research Quarterly*, 1968, *3*, 499-545.

Davis, F. B. Psychometric research on comprehension in reading. *Reading Research Quarterly*, 1972, *7*, 628-678.

Dooling, D. J., & Lachman, R. Effects of comprehension on retention of prose. *Journal of Experimental Psychology*, 1971, *88*, 216-222.

Drahozal, E. C., & Hanna, G. S. Reading comprehension subscores: Pretty bottles for ordinary wine. *Journal of Reading*, 1978, *21*, 416-420.

Echternacht, G. J. The use of confidence testing in objective tests. *Review of Educational Research*, 1972, *42*, 217-236.

Ericson, K.A., & Simon, H.A. Verbal reports as data. *Psychological Review*, 1980, *87*, 215-251.

Farr, R., & Tuinman, J. J. The dependent variable: Measurement issues in reading research. *Reading Research Quarterly*, 1972, *7*, 413-423.

Flavell, J. H., & Wellman, H. M. Metamemory. In R. V. Kail & J. W. Hagen (Eds.), *Perspectives on the development of memory and cognition*. Hillsdale, New Jersey: Erlbaum, 1977.

Frederiksen, C. H. Acquisiton of semantic information from discourse: Effects of repeated exposures. *Journal of Verbal Learning and Verbal Behavior*, 1975, *14*, 158-169.

Freebody, P. *Effects of vocabulary difficulty and text characteristics on children's reading comprehension*. Unpublished doctoral dissertation, University of Illinois, September 1980.

Gearhart, M., & Hall, W. S. *Internal state words: Cultural and situational variation in vocabulary usage* (Tech. Rep. No. 115). Urbana: University of Illinois, Center for the Study of Reading, February 1979. (ED 165 131)

Goetz, E. T., Anderson, R. C., & Schallert, D. L. *The representation of sentences in memory* (Tech. Rep. No. 144). Urbana: University of Illinois, Center for the Study of Reading, September 1979. (ED 177 527)

Goodman, K. S. *The psycholinguistic nature of the reading process*. Detroit: Wayne State University Press, 1968.

Green, G. M. *Organization, goals, and comprehensibility in narratives: Newswriting, a case study* (Tech. Rep. No. 132). Urbana: University of Illinois, Center for the Study of Reading, July 1979. (ED 174 949)

Green, G. M., & Laff, M. O. *Five-year-olds' recognition of authorship by literary style* (Tech. Rep. No. 181). Urbana: University of Illinois, Center for the Study of Reading, September 1980.

Greene, E. B. Achievement and confidence on true-false tests of college students. *Journal of Abnormal and Social Psychology*, 1929, *23*, 467-478.

Grice, H. P. Logic and conversation. In P. Cole and J. L. Morgan (Eds.), *Syntax and semantics: Speech acts* (Vol. 3). New York: Acadmic Press, 1975.

Grimes, J. *The thread of discourse*. The Hague: Mouton, 1975.

Guthrie, J. T. Models of reading disability. *Journal of Eductional Psychology*, 1973, *65*, 9-18.

Hall, W. S. *Testing for competence: Changing the criterion* (Working Paper No. 4, Part 1). New York: Rockefeller University Laboratory of Comparative

Human Cognition and the Institute of Comparative Human Development, 1977.

Hall, W. S., Reder, S., & Cole, M. Story recall in young black and white children: Effects of racial group membership, race of experimenter, and dialect. *Developmental Psychology*, 1975, *11*, 828-834.

Hall, W. S., & Tirre, W. C. *The communicative environment of young children: Social class, ethnic, and situational differences* (Tech. Rep. No. 125). Urbana: University of Illinois, Center for the Study of Reading, May 1979. (ED 170 788)

Hansen, J. The effects of inference training and practice on young children's reading comprehension. *Reading Research Quarterly*, 1981, *16*, 391-417.

Hanna, G. S., & Oaster, T. R. Toward a unified theory of context dependence. *Reading Research Quarterly*, 1978, *14*, 226-243.

Johnson, R. E. Abstractive processes in the remembering of prose. *Journal of Educational Psycholgy*, 1974, *66*, 772-779.

Kantor, R. N. Anomaly, inconsiderateness, and linguistic competence. In D. Gulstad (Ed.), *Papers from the 1977 Mid-Atlantic Linguistics Conference*. Columbia: University of Missouri, 1978.

Kavale, K., & Schreiner, R. The reading processes of above average and average readers: A comparison of the use of reasoning strategies in responding to standardized comprehension measures. *Reading Research Quarterly*, 1979, *15*, 102-128.

Keogh, B. K., & Margolis, J. Learn to labor and to wait: Attention problems of children with learning disorders. *Journal of Learning Disabilities*, 1976, *9*, 276-282.

Kintsch, W., & Keenan, J. Reading rate and retention as a function of the number of propositions on the base structure of sentences. *Cognitive Psychology*, 1973, *5*, 257-274.

Kintsch, W., Kozminsky, E., Streby, W. J., McKoon, G., & Keenan, J. M. Comprehension and recall of text as a function of content variables. *Journal of Verbal Learning and Verbal Behavior*, 1975, *14*, 196-214.

Kintsch, W., & van Dijk, T. A. Toward a model of text comprehension and production. *Psychological Review*, 1978, *85*, 363-394.

Labov, W. *Language in the inner city: Studies in the Black English Vernacular*. Philadelphia: University of Pennsylvania Press, 1972.

Lahey, B. B., McNees, M. P., & Brown, C. C. Modification of deficits in reading for comprehension. *Journal of Applied Behavior Analysis*, 1973, *6*, 475-480.

Lucas, P. A., & McConkie, G. W. The definition of test items: A descriptive approach. *American Educational Research Journal*, 1980, *17*, 133-140.

Lumsden, J. Test theory. *Annual Review of Psychology*, 1976, *27*, 251-280.

Mandler, J. M., & Johnson, N. S. Remembrance of things parsed: Story structure and recall. *Cognitive Psychology*, 1977, *9*, 111-151.

Markman, E. M. Realizing that you don't understand: Elementary school children's awareness of inconsistencies. *Child Development*, 1979, *50*, 643-655.

Marshall, N., & Glock, M. D. Comprehension of connected discourse: A study into the relationships between the structure of text and information recalled. *Reading Research Quarterly*, 1978, *14*, 10-56.

McConkie, G. Learning from text. *Review of Research in Education*, 1978, *5*, 3-48.

McConkie, G. W., Hogaboam, T. W., Wolverton, G. S., Zola, D., & Lucas, P. A. *Toward the use of eye movements in the study of language processing* (Tech. Rep. No. 134). Urbana: University of Illinois, Center for the Study of Reading, August 1979. (ED 174 968)

McConkie, G. W., Rayner, K., & Wilson, S. J. Experimental manipulation of reading strategies. *Journal of Educational Psychology*, 1973, *65*, 1-8.

Meyer, B. J. F. *The organization of prose and its effect on memory.* The Hague: Mouton, 1975.

Millman, J., Bishop, C. H., & Ebel, R. An analysis of test-wiseness. *Educational and Psychological Measurement*, 1965, *25*, 707-726.

Minsky, M. A framework for representing knowledge. In P. H. Winston (Ed.), *The psychology of computer vision.* New York: McGraw-Hill, 1975.

Myers, M., & Paris, S. Children's metacognitive knowledge about reading. *Journal of Educational Psychology*, 1978, *70*, 680-690.

Newsome, R. S., & Gaite, J. H. Prose learning: Effects of pretesting and reduction of passage length. *Psychological Reports*, 1971, *28*, 128-129.

Nicholls, J. G. Quality and equality in intellectual development: The role of motivation in education. *American Psychologist*, 1979, *34*, 1071-1084.

Norman, D. A., & Bobrow, D. G. On data-limited and resource limited processes. *Cognitive Psychology*, 1975, *7*, 44-66.

Olshavsky, J. E. Reading as problem solving: An investigation of strategies. *Reading Research Quarterly*, 1977, *12*, 654-674.

Omanson, R. C. *The narrative analysis.* Unpublished doctoral dissertation, University of Minnesota, 1979.

Omanson, R. C., Warren, W. H., & Trabasso, T. Goals, inferential comprehension and recall of stories by children. *Discourse Processes*, 1978, *1*, 337-354.

Ortony, A. *Some psycholinguistic aspects of metaphor* (Tech. Rep. No. 112). Urbana: University of Illinois, Center for the Study of Reading, January 1979. (ED 165 115)

Otto, W., Barrett, J. C., & Koenke, K. Assessment of children's statements of the main idea in reading. *Proceedings of the International Reading Association*, 1969, *13*, 692-697.

Paivio, A. *Imagery and verbal processes.* New York: Holt, Rinehart & Winston, 1971.

Paris, S. C., & Upton, L. R. Children's memory for inferential relationships in prose. *Child Development*, 1976, *47*, 660-668.

Pearson, P. D., & Johnson, D. D. *Teaching reading comprehension.* New York: Holt, Rinehart & Winston, 1978.

Pellegrino, J. W., & Glaser, R. Components of inductive reasoning. In R. Snow, P. A. Fedinco, & W. Montague (Eds.), *Aptitude, learning and instruction: Cognitive process analysis.* Hillsdale, New Jersey: Erlbaum, in press.

Pflaum, S. W., & Pascarella, E. T. Interactive effects of prior reading achievement and training in context on the reading of learning disabled children. *Reading Research Quarterly*, 1980, *16*, 138-158.

Pugh, R. C., & Brunza, J. J. Effects of a confidence weighted scoring system on measures of test reliability and validity. *Educational and Psychological Measurement*, 1975, *35*, 73-78.

Pyrczak, F. A responsive note on measures of the passage dependence of reading comprehension test items. *Reading Research Quarterly*, 1975-76, *11*, 112-117.

Raphael, T. E., Winograd, P., & Pearson, P. D. Strategies children use in answering questions. *Twenty-Ninth Yearbook of National Reading Conference*, in press.

Reynolds, R. E., & Anderson, R. C. *Influence of questions on the allocation of attention during reading* (Tech. Rep. No. 183). Urbana: University of Illinois, Center for the Study of Reading, October 1980.

Reynolds, R. E., Standiford, S. N., & Anderson, R. C. *Distribution of reading time when questions are asked about a restricted category of text* (Tech. Rep. No. 83). Urbana: University of Illinois, Center for the Study of Reading, April 1978. (ED 153 206)

Rosenblatt, L. M. *The reader, the text, the poem: The transactional theory of the literary work*. Carbondale, Illinois: Southern Illinois University Press, 1978.

Royer, J. M., & Cable, G. W. Facilitated learning in connected discourse. *Journal of Educational Psychology*, 1975, *67*, 116-123.

Royer, J. M., & Cunningham, D. J. *On the theory and measurement of reading comprehension* (Tech. Rep. No. 91). Urbana: University of Illinois, Center for the Study of Reading, June 1978. (ED 157 040)

Rumelhart, D. E. Understanding and summarizing brief stories. In D. LaBerge & J. Samuels (Eds.), *Basic processes in reading: Perception and comprehension*. Hillsdale, New Jersey: Erlbaum, 1977.

Rumelhart, D. D., & Ortony, A. The representation of knowledge in memory. In R. C. Anderson, R. J. Spiro, & W. E. Montague (Eds.), *Schooling and the acquistion of knowledge*. Hillsdale, New Jersey: Erlbaum, 1977.

Rystrom, R. Toward defining comprehension: A second report. *Journal of Reading Behavior*, 1970, *2*, 144-157.

Sarnacki, R. E. Examination of test wiseness in the cognitive test domain. *Review of Educational Research*, 1979, *49*, 252-279.

Seigler, R. S. Developmental sequences within and between concepts. *Monographs of the Society for Research in Child Development*, in press.

Schank, R. C. The structure of episodes in memory. In D. G. Bobrow & A. Collins (Eds.), *Representation and understanding: Studies in cognitive science*. New York: Academic Press, 1975.

Schank, R. C., & Abelson, R. P. *Scripts, plans, goals and understanding*. Hillsdale, New Jersey: Erlbaum, 1977.

Slakter, M. J., Koehler, R. A., & Hampton, S. H. Grade level, sex and selected aspects of test-wiseness. *Journal of Educational Measurement*, 1970, *7*, 247-254.

Spearitt, D. Identification of subskills of reading comprehension by maximum likelihood factor analysis. *Reading Research Quarterly*, 1972, *8*, 92-111.

Spielberger, C. D., Anton, W. D., & Bedell, J. The nature and treatment of test anxiety. In M. Zuckerman & C. D. Spielberger (Eds.), *Emotions and anxiety: New concepts, methods and applications*. Hillsdale, New Jersey: Erlbaum, 1976.

Spiro, R. J. *Inferential reconstruction in memory for connected discourse* (Tech. Rep. No. 2). Urbana: University of Illinois, Center for the Study of Reading, October 1975. (ED 136 187)

Spiro, R. J. *Schema theory and reading comprehension: New directions* (Tech. Rep. No. 191). Urbana: University of Illinois, Center for the Study of Reading, December 1980.

Steffensen, M. S., & Guthrie, L. F. *Effects of situation on the verbalization of black inner-city children* (Tech. Rep. No. 180). Urbana: University of Illinois, Center for the Study of Reading, September 1980.

Steffensen, M. S., Reynolds, R. C., McClure, E., & Guthrie, L. F. *Black English Vernacular and reading comprehension: A cloze study of third, sixth, and ninth graders* (Tech. Rep. No. 199). Urbana: University of Illinois, Center for the Study of Reading, February 1981.

Stein, N. L., & Glenn, C. G. An analysis of story comprehension in elementary school children. In R. O. Freedle (Ed.), *Discourse processing: Multidisciplinary perspective*. Norwood, New Jersey: Ablex, 1978.

Stein, N. L., & Nezworski, T. *The effects of organization and instructional set* on *story memory* (Tech. Rep. No. 68). Urbana: University of Illinois, Center for the Study of Reading, January 1978. (ED 149 327)

Sternberg, R. J. *Intelligence, information processing, and analogical reasoning: The componential analysis of human abilities.* Hillsdale, New Jersey: Erlbaum, 1977.

Thorndike, E. L. Reading as reasoning: A Study of mistakes in paragraph reading. *Journal of Educational Research, 1917, 8,* 323-332.

Thorndike, P. Cognitive structures in comprehension and memory of narrative discourse. *Cognitive Psychology,* 1977, *9,* 77-110.

Thorndike, R. L. Reading as reasoning. *Reading Research Quarterly,* 1974, *9,* 137-147.

Tierney, R. J., & LaZansky, J. *The rights and responsibilities of readers and writers: A contractual agreement* (Reading Education Rep. No. 15). Urbana: University of Illinois, Center for the Study of Reading, January 1980. (ED 181 447)

Trabasso, T. *On the making of inferences during reading and their assessment* (Tech. Rep. No. 157). Urbana: University of Illinois, Center for the Study of Reading, January 1980. (ED 181 429)

Tuinman, J. J. Determining the passage-dependency of comprehension questions in 5 major tests. *Reading Research Quarterly,* 1974, *9,* 207-223.

Tuinman, J. J. Reading is recognition—When reading is not reasoning. In J. C. Harste & R. R. Carey (Eds.), *New perspectives on comprehension* (Monograph in Language and Reading Studies No. 3). Bloomington: Indiana University, 1979, 38-48.

Tulving, E. Relationship between encoding specificity and levels of processing. In L. S. Cermak & F. I. M. Craik (Eds.), *Levels of processing and human memory.* Hillsdale, New Jersey: Erlbaum, 1978.

van Dijk, T. A. Semantic macro-structures and knowledge frames in discourse comprehension. In M. A. Just & P. A. Carpenter (Eds.), *Cognitive processes in comprehension.* Hillsdale, New Jersey: Erlbaum, 1977.

Venezky, R. L. *Testing in reading: Assessment and instructional decisionmaking.* National Council of Teachers of English and ERIC Clearinghouse on Reading and Communication Skills, 1974.

Vernon, P. E. The determinants of reading comprehension. *Educational and Psychological Measurement,* 1962, *22,* 269-286.

Vygotsky, L. S. *Mind in society: The development of higher psychological processes.* M. Cole, V. John-Steiner, S. Scribner, & E. Souberman (Eds. & Trans.). Cambridge, Massachusetts: Harvard University Press, 1978.

Wahlstrom, M., & Boersma, F. J. The influence of test-wiseness upon achievement. *Educational and Psychological Measurement,* 1968, *28,* 413-420.

Warren, W. H., Nicholas, D. N., & Trabasso, T. Event chains and inferences in understanding narratives. In R. Freedle (Ed.), *New directions in discourse processing: Advances in discourse processes* (Vol. 2). Hillsdale, New Jersey: Erlbaum, 1979.

Washington, E. D. *The classification of reading comprehension test items and its relation to the performance of selected racial groups.* Unpublished doctoral dissertation, University of Iowa, July 1979.

Weiner, B. *Theories of motivation: From mechanism to cognition.* Chicago: Markhan, 1972.

Winograd, P., & Johnston, P. *Comprehension monitoring and the error detection paradigm* (Tech. Rep. No. 153). Urbana: University of Illinois, Center for the Study of Reading, January 1980. (ED 181 425)

Yendovitskaya, T.V. Development of memory. In A. V. Saparozhets & D. B. Elkonin (Eds.), *The psychology of preschool children.* Cambridge, Massachusetts: M.I.T. Press, 1971.